EIVIND BERGGRAV, GOD'S MAN OF SUSPENSE

Eivind Berggrav

God's Man of Suspense

by

ALEX JOHNSON

translated by

KJELL JORDHEIM

with

HARRIET L. OVERHOLT

AUGSBURG PUBLISHING HOUSE

Minneapolis, Minnesota

This volume is a translation of the Norwegian book *Eivind Berggrav, Spenningens Mann,* published in 1959 by Land og Kirke, Oslo, Norway.

Manufactured in the United States of America

Preface

Two circumstances have made it possible for this biography to be written such a short time after the death of Bishop Eivind Berggrav on January 14, 1959.

First, my acquaintance with the Bishop's family is of long standing. Berggrav became acquainted with my father as a high school student, and since then our families have been friends for two or three generations. Kathrine and Eivind Berggrav were often in my childhood home. The friendship continued after my father's death; and my mother and I often enjoyed long visits at the Berggravs, both in Hurdal and in Tromsø. From 1937 on, Berggrav was my bishop in Oslo, with close cooperation between us. This friendship has provided me with an abundance of memories.

Second, I have had access to the papers that
Bishop Berggrav left. There are bound collections
of reprints of his articles and big albums of newspaper clippings. I have read—besides his books—
the unpublished memoirs of his childhood and
youth, his visitation reports, and other manuscripts.
These I could check with the clippings and reprints.
For access to these papers I owe his family many
thanks.

I wish also to thank Pastors Alf Hauge and
Henrik Hauge, who helped me with information
about Berggrav's work in the Bible Society and in
the Ecumenical Movement. My gratitude goes out
also to those who have told me of any episode about
Eivind Berggrav that should be remembered.

ALEX JOHNSON

Contents

EIVIND JOSEF BERGGRAV

Born October 25, 1884, in Stavanger.

Candidatus theologiae, University of Oslo, 1909.

Married Kathrine Seip, 1909.

Teacher, Eidsvoll Folk High School, 1909-1914.

Headmaster, Holmestrand Teachers' College, 1914-1915.

Editor, "Kirke og Kultur" Magazine, 1915-1959.

Published his first book, *Krigerliv og religiøsitet*, 1915.

Principal, Akershus Provincial College, 1915-1918.

Rector, Hurdal Parish, 1919-1925.

Doctor of Theology *honoris causa*, Lund University, Sweden, 1923.

Doctor of Theology *in cursu*, University of Oslo, 1925.

Bishop of Hålogaland, 1929-1937.

Bishop of Oslo, 1937-1951.

Imprisoned by Nazis, 1942-1945.

Grand Cross, Order of St. Olav, 1947.

Author of more than forty-five books (listed at end of this volume).

Died January 14, 1959, in Oslo.

Chapter One

Man of Tensions

IN 1928 in one of Oslo's churches Bishop Eivind Berggrav was officiating at the marriage of a couple that he knew well. The groom gives us this account of what happened:

On the day before our wedding I was taken ill, and it was arranged that both bride and groom should be seated for most of the ceremony. The sexton was new and visibly nervous, for he had never before assisted in a ceremony where the bridal pair were seated. At one point in the service we rose and remained standing for a time. When we went to sit down again, the sexton pulled out the bride's chair in such a way that she fell flat on the floor.

Bishop Berggrav was facing the altar. As quickly as possible the bride got to her feet, and Berggrav ceremoniously turned to face us, the Altar Book still in his hand. Then slowly, as if it were a part of the ritual, he said, "When King Olav first landed on the coast of Norway, he slipped and fell. Then said Rane, the king's fosterchild, 'Now you have taken foothold in this country, my Lord and King.' The same thing is true for you, Elsebeth. Now you have taken foothold in the

1

new state which you are entering. And this fall shall be a
token of good fortune for you."

The audience gasped in alarm and admiration, and the
ceremony continued as if nothing had happened.

It is a part of the story that afterward at the wedding
dinner, when all the other speeches had been given, Berggrav
rose and proposed a toast to "the unhappiest man in the
world today—our sexton."

*   *   *

So it is that we remember Bishop Berggrav—a
man full of life and full of surprises. He knew how
to find a way out. He was quick to prevent people
from being hurt. He seemed to have read everything, to know everything, and to be able always
to put what he knew to work at the right moment.

There are, of course, those who might think that
such a cleverly resourceful person would be flighty
or unstable. There seemed to be no limit to the
things Berggrav could turn his hands to, and he
also had a strange faculty for being on the spot
when and where things were happening.

He could be in Norway one day, and the next day
in America. One day might find him at the Acade-
my of Science, and the next speaking at a meeting
for alcoholics. He could be a caller at the King's
palace one hour, and shortly afterward be found
deep in conversation with a poor fellow in prison.
He was equally at ease as a speaker at a revival
meeting for missions and as an opponent at a

doctoral disputation. He could write Bible history for school children and learned literary reviews almost simultaneously. He could talk law with lawyers and medicine with doctors.

Thus one could go on enumerating his activities. But one must also add that in spite of the demanding positions he held and filled surpassingly well, he was always close to his family, and this in an era when fathers often had little attention to give to home life.

It is indeed true that he was an astonishingly versatile man. He was a person of unusual dimensions, with swift intelligence and wide-ranging talents, possessed of an enormous capacity for work, and with a kind of self-discipline that enabled him to make use of every available minute and every ounce of his energy.

Some will perhaps insist that the Bishop must have had some weaknesses, that no one human being could make such tremendous contributions to so many different fields.

There might easily have been weaknesses. He *might* have become flighty or unstable. He was a journalist of sorts, both in work and in temperament, and journalists with so many things to cover are sometimes inclined to become superficial.

But Berggrav was never superficial. His chief defense against flightiness or superficiality was his

simple Christian faith which never lost its hold on
him, even in the great crises of his religious life.
There was something incredibly simple and childlike in his Christianity. To this extent it may be
true, as some have said, that the Bishop was no
theologian—that is, if to be a theologian means to
make religion complicated.

Berggrav could not live without a clear, direct
relationship with God. To hear him pray in a small
group was an unforgettable experience. He talked
to God like a child, openly, and without a shadow
of a doubt.

Not long before his death, when he was confined
to his home, he learned about a woman in Uranienborg who was ill and depressed. In his grace at the
breakfast table he used to pray for many people,
mentioning them by name. ("I take all the time I
want when I pray," he often said.) On this particular morning he said quite simply, "And now,
dear God, please give some joy to Aud today."

In the afternoon he heard that it had happened.
A friend had come to see Aud, bringing her a big
azalea. Then Berggrav folded his hands, "Thank
you, dear God, for the azalea." There was not the
least doubt in his simple soul as to how this had
come about.

His life was filled with such things. He dwelt in
a living world where God was always on the go,

everywhere, so that it was a daily source of excitement to keep up with all that God was doing.

This childlike relationship with God was the very core of his life. And so it was hard on him when his soul suffered the "winterdark days" that he wrote about in his book, *Sanctification*.

Because he was childlike in faith, he could be many-sided but not superficial. Because inwardly he was simple and strong, he could embrace so much and reach so far. Yet between these two facets of his nature there was not harmony but tension.

Berggrav loved that word *suspense,* using it over and over again. He was indeed *spenningens mann*—that is, a man of suspense and of great intensity.

In a letter to their children in 1944, his wife Kathrine—after 39 years of marriage—used the term to designate what seemed to her his most individual quality. She still found him exciting. He could come up with astonishing surprises and boyish pranks. But she also used the expression with a deeper meaning: to denote an inner intensity in his person.

Others felt the same way about him and used similar terms to express their feelings. It seems, moreover, appropriate to designate the author of the popular book *Land of Suspense,* as a man of suspense.

He was sometimes tense almost to the breaking

point, strained not only between simplicity and complexity, but also between loneliness and fellowship. Sometimes even in the finest company he would become completely withdrawn, lost in his own thought. Then, before long, he would *have* to have someone to talk to. He could find himself again in immediate, confiding contact with others. He was usually impelled to action, not by solitude but by fellowship. It was he who founded our Christian Council, and both the name and the cause have become part of the imperishable heritage of our church.

One of Berggrav's books, *Humor and Gravity,* suggests still another area of conflict and tension. Regarding it, he once said:

That soberness which cannot smile at a joke is not good, but worse still is the joke that is not based on some sense.

Many other contrasts could be cited, such as Berggrav's critical attitude toward certain men, which again and again was offset by an almost naive sympathy, especially toward those he had once criticized. But sharpest of all was the contrast between his critical self-appraisal on the one hand and on the other an impulsive spontaneity that was sometimes almost shocking.

"It just popped out," he said once with a conciliatory smile when he was called to account for his famous remark about the Inner Mission to the effect that it could "slay many peeping sprouts of Christian faith." And it was true; he often just "popped off" about things. One could fill pages about times when Berggrav blurted out opinions that others would have phrased more discreetly. Sometimes his popping-off relieved the situation; sometimes it hurt; but it was never malicious or spiteful. He always knew what he was saying, and he meant what he said. His remark about the tender sprouts was, as he admitted later, an over-statement; but it was born of one of his fundamental principles: he wanted to be a minister to those who were seeking; he wanted to foster the slow growth, the shy Christian life, perhaps because that had been his kind of faith for so many years.

There is truth, too, in the comment—made, for example, in the *Norwegian Mission Tidings*—that Berggrav was the *boy* among our churchmen. Boy-like, he was never sarcastic in his speech, but only outspoken. But we must remember also that this boy had always been a man, that he had been grown up even as a child, and for that reason he could remain a child as an adult. "For years," he wrote to his wife, November 24, 1943, "we long to really grow up, but we never quite do. We only grow older!"

In spite of his impulsiveness, Berggrav always knew what he was doing. It was as if he kept one

eye trained on himself and was forever burdened
with the responsibility of keeping track of himself. Was that one reason he was often so boyish?
Was he trying to escape from his own watchful
eye?

We all know something about this feeling. At
times we are impulsive and let ourselves go; at
other times we are watchful of our actions. But we
are not both at the same time; or at the most we
are halfway impulsive and halfway reflective. Now,
it would not have been too bad to be Eivind Berggrav if he had been such a half-and-half person.
But then he could never have become the man he
was. What underlay all his problems and all his
achievements was the fact that he was at all times,
simultaneously, completely impulsive and completely reflective, and that he knew this to be the
case.

We may consider these two temperaments to be
as incompatible as fire and water. But Eivind Berggrav seems to have been exceptional in this respect.
We do know that when fire and water come together, there is an explosion of sorts. And it is
certainly true that Berggrav's life was explosive,
marked by frequent eruptions of his conflicting
tensions.

Once we understand these conflicts, we have the
key to Berggrav's nature—to such paradoxical

traits as his gentle sensitivity and his often blunt manner of speaking. We have the key also to his incredible activity and to that lively energy which impressed all who met him. There can be no mental lassitude when the mind is tensed between action and reflection. Faculties will be stretched to their utmost and the lively spirit will find relief only in action. Herein lies the key to Berggrav's resourcefulness, to his assurance that there was always a way out, and to his facility in finding right solutions.

Could anyone be happy living with such inner conflicts and tensions?

Perhaps the word *happiness* has taken on some Hollywood connotations which can hardly be applied to Berggrav. But he was certainly not unhappy. There was a great deal of joy in his life, probably more than in the lives of most ministers. His joy found expression not only in lively conversation, in good stories, in jubilant companionship with God and men, but above all in profound gratitude. Berggrav was content to have found his right niche in life—a calling in which he could make good use of all his faculties. He was most happy in his marriage and in his family life. His deepest emotion, powerful to resolve all tensions, was his abounding gratitude.

At the same time, evil was ever lurking at his

side. In his address to the Lutheran World Convention in Hannover in 1952, his main point, clearly
stated, was this: *There is a foe*. Berggrav knew this
foe, the enemy of happiness in life and of peace
with God. He had had his own dark hours of conflict with this spiritual adversary. But he also knew
the way to victory:

> His rage we can endure,
> For lo! his doom is sure.
> One little word shall fell him.

And so Berggrav could be glad even in his dark-
est hours. In all his conflicts he was striving for
harmony. He knew that it was there and that some
day he would find it. He possessed it only in hope-
ful anticipation, but his hope was firm as the rock.

Berggrav was not a man without faults. But I
have never known a man who could face his weaknesses so frankly. He was especially critical of what
he considered his worst thorn-in-the-flesh—his pre-
occupation with himself. He fought against all his
failings, fought even if he felt the victory would
not be won in this life, fought the harder the lower
he seemed to fall. His Christian faith was a vital
necessity in the struggle. He was jubilantly happy
each time it lifted him up again into fellowship
with God and man.

He was a good soldier, a man of tensions and
intensity.

Chapter Two

His Father, His Ideal

"YOUR father is the prototype of your life," Oscar Pfister told Eivind Berggrav in the middle 1920's when Eivind was about to undergo psychoanalysis by this famous disciple of Freud. The analysis was part of an educational program, but in Berggrav's case it was never completed. It felt, as he himself later expressed it, as though a chill wind accompanied this "operation on the soul."

Nevertheless, he admitted that Pfister was right in the observation about his father, and he made reference to it in an address delivered on September 1, 1956, on the occasion of the 100th anniversary of the birth of his father, Bishop and Doctor of Theology Otto Jensen.

Berggrav had originally consented to the psychoanalysis partly because as a Doctor of Theology in

religious psychology, he wanted to know what this
new type of analysis was like; and he was annoyed
at the "scientific muzzle" that psychoanalysts were
putting on those who had not been analyzed. A
second reason was that Berggrav wanted to understand himself. Of course, he had always been interested in observing himself, and he had realized
early what an important influence his father had
had on his life.

He often called attention to their parallel roles.
Both were theologians; both had begun as teachers
and then had become pastors. "He was just like
me," Berggrav wrote. "We both received our doctor's degrees in our 41st year; both were about to
become professors, and both substituted in the same
professorship at the University; but neither one of
us was a real scholar."

We may question that last statement, but the
others are facts. And the similarities can be continued. Both became bishops; and although only the
father became a Cabinet member, the son was twice
offered a Cabinet seat. Probably one reason that
Berggrav refused the offers was that his father had
felt somewhat uneasy and unhappy during his term
in the Cabinet.

Both men were active in the language controversy
of the times; both were openminded toward the
stormy advances of natural science; both were more

moved by Grundtvig's popular approach than by
Gisle Johnson's pietism; both were men of the
Church-at-large rather than supporters of any
particular sectarian movement.

In the story of his life which Berggrav prepared
when he was ordained as bishop, he expressed his
feelings for his father in these words: "I had im-
measurable respect for my father, though it was
not inspired by anything in his outward manner.
To Mother and us children, he was our sunshine.
In my youth my mainspring of action was a burning desire to win my father's respect; and later
when Father and I met as men and theologians, we
experienced a mutual understanding and affection,
which on my part was always intensified by my
genuine reverence for him. As a father, as a theologian, and as a Christian, he has been the guiding
influence of my life. I shall never be anything more
than his son."

If the last sentence seems something of an exag-
geration, we must remember that this was back in
1929, and Eivind Berggrav was at that time pretty
much a newcomer in our church. He had ranked
only third in the number of votes cast in the
bishops' election, although he was first choice in
the pastors' votes; and he had not been recom-
mended by any of the bishops. Yet he became
bishop; and no one was more aware than he of the

importance to him of the pattern set for him by
his father.

Otto Jensen had not been a stern father, but he
believed that children should never be praised in
their own hearing. The story of Berggrav's first
printed article is a case in point. It was a long newspaper article, captioned, "Some Words to the
Orthodox, by a Young Man." Eivind had written
it and sent it in anonymously to the *Stavanger Af-
tenblad* (Evening Paper). He was then about 18
years old and in his last year of junior college
(Gymnasium). The article appeared on December
12, 1902. The editor, Lars Oftedal, was one of
those who, 26 years later, was to help make Eivind
a bishop.

Eivind was most anxious to know what his
father's opinion of the article would be, but he was
afraid to let the family know that he was the
anonymous author. There was a surprise in store
for him. Eight days later his mother came into his
room in the evening to tell him that she and his
father had realized that he was the author, that his
father was very happy and had sent the article to
Pastor Klaveness. The pastor later wrote the young
student thanking him for the article. But Otto
Jensen never said one word to his son about it,
neither then nor later.

This reticence on the part of father and son did

not spring, as we might suppose, from any kind of authority imposed by the father. It was the result of a shyness characteristic of both men. One could not talk about the big things that happened—and it was a big thing for a young man of 18 and his proud father that such an article had appeared in print.

Although, as Berggrav wrote later, desire for his father's approval was the "mainspring of action" for all he did in his youth, it is likely that the boy never heard one word of appreciation from his father directly.

On one occasion he did receive encouragement indirectly. He was 14 at the time and living in Asak, where his father was the pastor from 1889 to 1899. The father was standing on the porch steps talking to the doctor, and Eivind was at an alcove window just above. They were talking about him, and Eivind heard his father say, "That boy is always busy with something. He is full of projects. He will certainly amount to something!"

During World War II, while Berggrav was held a Nazi prisoner at Bredtvedt, he occupied his time by writing memoirs of his childhood. In them he said, "Nothing in my life has meant more to me than my father's words to Dr. Hougland that day. They made an opening in the barrier that seemed to separate my father and me. Now I had a secret

channel to him." He goes on to say that he could
embellish the statement with flowery rhetoric,
mentioning the honors that had come to him, yet it
would still be true. He did not make more of the
story because he did not want to appear to be a
show-off.

But the point of the incident is not the ambition
of the boy, or the honors that came to him. It lies
in the value he set upon the close relationship it gave
him with his father—the secret channel to him.
This feeling he kept the rest of his life, except that
it did not remain a secret channel. With maturity,
there developed an ideal relationship between them
—a friendly bond between two men and two theologians. The belief that real *intimacy* develops
from some *separation* is one of the things that Berggrav learned from his relationship with his father.

Berggrav's mother, Maren Christine Jensen, was
the person the children went to when they were in
trouble. Warm-hearted, impulsive, gentle, she was
mediator and moderator for them. She knew how
to combine firmness with freedom in bringing up
children. "Rightness and goodness belonged together with Mother," Berggrav said of her.

Otto Jensen was a high school teacher in Stavanger when his oldest son Eivind Josef was born there
on October 25, 1884. Otto was a natural teacher
and educator—a gift he inherited from his father,

Even Jensen. Born at Norderhov, Even had spent most of his working years at Kongsberg, where he was a school principal and a parish clerk and sexton. His wife (and Otto's mother), Inger Margrethe Berggrav,* was also an educator.

Berggrav owed a good deal to his grandfather (Even Jensen). Dr. Halvdan Koht, the famous historian and political figure, once asked Berggrav, "Who really had the best head, Bishop Eivind Berggrav; his father, Bishop Otto Jensen; or the old grandfather and sexton at Kongsberg?" Berggrav replied that without the shadow of a doubt it was grandfather!

After ten years in Asak, Eivind's family moved back to Stavanger, and it was there the boy received his Bachelor of Arts degree in 1903. He received "firsts" in his written subjects, and he has said that his first thought when the marks were announced was, "If only Grandfather had lived to see this day!" Even Jensen had died in March of that year. The young graduate was glad, though, that Grandfather did not know about the C in

---

*It was through this grandmother that Eivind Berggrav got his family name. Otto Jensen had considered changing his own name. He was born and raised in Kongsberg, where his mother's family name was well and honorably known. He owed much to his mother, a great, warm-hearted person, and he resembled her in type and temperament. But out of regard for his father, he did not change his name. However, he urged his children to make the change. At first they called themselves Berggrav-Jensen; but when the government would no longer legalize double names, the sons of Otto Jensen were given permission to use the name Berggrav.

oral French, which somewhat dimmed the luster
of the series of "firsts."

Berggrav was not only proud of his family, he
was trying to live up to its traditions and fulfill its
expectations of him. The thought was not so much
a spur as an inspiration to the young man. Certainly he often wondered what father or grandfather
would have said about one thing or another that he
had done—sometimes with pleasure at the thought,
sometimes with embarrassment. He could always
see his life against a backdrop of the past. It was
part of his destiny and a source of gratitude within
him.

His affectionate relationship with his father
reached full-blown maturity. The men had their
last talk together about 10 days before the death
of the father in 1918. Berggrav was then 35 years
old, but he writes, "No little child ever appreciated
more the joy of having a father and a mother than
I did at that time." It was Sunday, and Berggrav
had gone to hear his father preach in Hamar Cathedral. He was so moved by the sermon that he had
to leave the church and be alone for a while. He
had never heard such a sermon before in all his life.
Now at last he could confess it himself: Christ was
truly the Son of God.

That sermon and the talk with his father that
followed it became the turning point in Berggrav's

life. As a result of it he too decided to become a
minister. He made the final decision in the *Aula*
(Concourse) of the University at the anniversary
festival on September 2 of that same year.

Pfister was right: Berggrav's father was his ideal.

Chapter Three

Doubt and Faith

BERGGRAV had at first intended to become an engineer, for he had considerable technological ability. Even as a boy he was adept in photography. This was so early in the development of photography that he had to prepare his own plates, and later he did his own developing and printing. At the age of 13 he made a hectograph and with it got out a newspaper of his own. He was always interested in the technical aspects of things.

So it was that in the fall of his fifteenth year he did some apprentice work in a shop in Stavanger; and when he entered the *Gymnasium**, natural sciences were his major subjects. He had graduated from Middle School at Halden, while his family was living in Asak. Now in high school he became "all

---

*A Norwegian *Gymnasium* is roughly equivalent to an American junior college.

fire and flame" over the sciences—especially biology, chemistry, and mathematics. He made himself a kind of chemistry laboratory in a big closet at home, receiving many tips from his teacher about the experiments he undertook. He was trying to improve upon or out-reach the experiments done in school. The teacher instinct was already showing itself in him.

In his personal philosophy, biology was influencing him the most. He says of himself that he "went from fact to fact, from proof to proof. One truth became evident: *There is a law of order ruling over everything.*" This realization awakened his doubts as to the accuracy of the Bible, especially in its account of the creation. Secretly he had already read many modernist attacks on Christianity while he was preparing for his confirmation, and he could not help agreeing with some of their arguments although his heart still clung to the faith of his childhood.

Then he was genuinely converted in true Stavanger fashion. This was in March, 1902, when he was 17. Now he really had a problem. He must find the bridge between faith and science; and never for a moment did he doubt that he could find it. He began reading the magazine, *Church and Culture,* and felt drawn to the editor, a parish minister named Klaveness, especially in the man's attempt to reconcile the old faith with the new science. At the same time he became ardently interested in the rising controversy within the church. For the very sake of one's faith, it seemed necessary to discuss these questions freely. This conviction became the subject of his first printed article. The whole controversy did not seem to disturb him at that time.

Instead he became an even more ardent Christian. He arranged for a series of Bible studies in his home under the leadership of Karl Ludwig Reichelt, then a student at the School of Missions. It was during this period that Berggrav's devotion to missions was awakened—a love that continued throughout his life, giving special significance to his ecumenical work.

It was after hearing a sermon by the missionary minister, Johannes Johnson, that Eivind made up his mind to become a pastor. On May 4, 1903, he told his father of his decision. The father's reaction was typical. After a moment of silence he said, "Then it is foolish for you to be majoring in natural science." It was the father's natural reticence at work; but the boy was deeply hurt to receive no word of joy or encouragement.

Upon his matriculation, the boy left for the Students' Home in Oslo, where he was to begin his theological studies. His father had made all the arrangements for him and Berggrav was deeply grateful. His actual entrance to the University was a moment of deep significance. It was early one morning late in August. All alone the boy entered the great hall of the *Domus Academica*. He was overwhelmed by the solemnity of the moment. Something within him intoned, "Holy is the call of the student." There in the center of the stone floor he knelt and asked God's blessing upon his student years.

His principal outside interest during his student years was the Norwegian Students' Christian Association. He had become acquainted with the organization in the summer of 1903 at the convention of Nordic students at Sorø. There he heard Olfert Ricard speak and was kindled by his enthusiasm; there he listened to Johannes Johnson's missionary appeal; and there he fell in love with Denmark, which was to become a second fatherland to him and his wife.

At that time the leaders in the organization were Professors Simon Michelet and Lyder Brun. But the inspiration came from the visits of John Mott and Robert Wilder. Young Berggrav was fired with enthusiasm by their rousing calls to prayer and missionary work. He prepared, among other things, a small printed pamphlet for the group, listing the things that members should ask for in their morning and evening prayers.

Two years later when the students met, first in Holland and later in Germany, Berggrav was one of the four delegates from Norway. The others were Volrath Vogt, Sten Bugge, and Kathrine Seip, whom he got to know on this trip.

At the meeting, the great moment came when John Mott made his plea for funds for the World-wide Student Movement. It was God Himself, Mott explained, who would provide the money—but through *their efforts*. Who could doubt it? Pads of paper were passed out to all the delegates. "And now," said Mott, "I will pray to God while you fill out your slips and set down the amount that you believe God can provide through you for the sake of His kingdom."

"It was a great moment," Berggrav has written. "At first I thought of 1,000 kroner,* but had come down to 200 when I glanced at Volrath Vogt's slip. I did not know a more earnest believer than Vogt. He had written 15! I wrote 50!"

We may be inclined to smile at the incident, but to Berggrav it was a serious matter. The ensuing pressure began slowly to undermine his faith.

It is interesting to see how Berggrav earned his money. At that time 50 kroner was a lot of money for a student; and even though Mott had said that

*The Norwegian *krone* is now worth about 21 cents in American money.

they were to pray for it, Berggrav knew it would take some doing on his part too. He saved a little out of his scant spending money, but he also earned some by acting as a barber during his summer vacation in Røldal where the summer tourists appreciated his services. And then his technical skill came to his assistance. He was very good at sharpening razors, and he earned the rest of his pledge to World Missions by keeping the razors of the summer guests in good shape.

In the depth of his soul this shy, tense young Norwegian student reacted strongly against Anglo-Saxon Methodism. This reaction, together with his studies, brought him slowly to a religious crisis which reached its climax in the spring of 1906. It seemed to him that philosophy and natural science gave Christianity the semblance of unreality.

For him it was a pure and simple intellectual doubt. Later Berggrav was much disturbed if anyone ever insisted that doubt always sprang from sin or from unwillingness to follow God's commandments. Of course, he knew that much doubt arose from certain moral issues and that the arguments of such doubters were only rationalizations of man's desire to live his life without God. But he knew too that there were exceptions to this rule. There are people who want to believe but who cannot do so, no matter how hard they try. It later became his chief desire to be a minister to these honest doubters. Many a time he took up the gauntlet for them; he could not, would not, ever fail to come to their aid. The reason is simple: For many years, from the time he was 22 until he was 35, he was one of them.

His doubt was basic, fundamental; and Berggrav watched with alarmed accuracy its slow growth. At first it was simply that he could no longer be on fire for any cause. He who a short time before had been the "steward for all right thinking" now sat and "was sorry because I could not see one cause genuine enough for me to get excited about." This was intelligence reacting against the flaming zeal that had carried him away in his first experience as a Christian.

From theologians he received little help. Even at that time he had dissociated himself from the liberal theology prevailing at the University. "The front of controversy between two theological viewpoints has never been my personal front," he said at his ordination. This was the situation during his University years, though as we have seen, it had been different when he was in the *Gymnasium*. Then his doubts were not so strong, and he found the concessions made by liberal theologians to science helpful.

But now no concessions helped. His problems now concerned not doubt over certain doctrines

but the actual question of God's existence. Was not
all religion an illusion born of man's fears and
dreams?

His very doubts tormented him doubly because
they were in accord with one pole of his tension-
torn inner self. In his diary from that period we
read:

> It is as if something within me has become visibly fright-
> ened or fearful. And I know what it is that has frightened
> me. It is all this *reflection* that has poured in over me lately,
> paralyzing all immediate and complete dedication. . . . I long
> to be more poor in spirit.

The quotation is typical of his self-observation,
of his inner conflicts, and especially of his spiritual
sense of dedication which in the end brought him
release.

But he still had a long way to go. By May 1906
he had decided that he could not become a pastor,
and his diary for June 11 has this record:

> It has happened. Not by anything outwardly. It is only that
> I know now that I am not and cannot be a Christian. It is
> as clear to me as a revelation.

It happened on his way home from a party where
he had been talking with C. J. Hambro. Berggrav
had not said a word to him about his own doubts,
but when they left each other, it seemed to Berggrav as if a physician had just told him that he was
about to die. He could not sleep. At last he could

stand it no longer. He got up, took a watering can
and went out into the yard, and there he poured
water over his naked body. When he came in again,
the hands on the wall clock showed exactly four
o'clock. He stood there inside the door, watching
the clock. "Something within me," he has said,
"seemed to say, 'At this hour your faith died. You
are now a free-thinker.' Everything felt empty and
still. It was quiet because the struggle was over. But
existence seemed plucked bare."

His doubts had brought an end to his religious
thinking. About the same time he went to communion for the last time for many years, perhaps
trying it as a last resort, but the hold of faith had
been broken. Now even his *feeling* for religion was
gone.

But it was not quite so bad as it seemed.

In the first place, the whole moral system of
Christianity seemed to him unassailable. No matter
what he believed, so far as conduct and behavior
were concerned, he would live like a Christian.
And he did. And then, he had not become a *rela-
tivist* as so many modern doubters had. Truth was
still majestic, absolute. It was his sense of truth that
had compelled him to admit that there was no God.
And finally, he continued going to church and reading the Bible. "So long as I keep my Bible free from
dust, there is clarity and quiet within me," he wrote

to Kathrine Seip to whom he had become engaged.

It seems as if almost as soon as he lost his faith he began groping his way back. At any rate he continued to search. If God did not exist, there was a whole cosmos to be explored. Without God, how was he to explain the coherence and harmony of existence?

One answer was plain: *causality*—the study of the relations between cause and effect—that should reveal the truth. In physics the matter was clear. It had been proved that the laws of cause worked illimitably and explained everything. But what about intellectual life? Was Taine right in assuming that virtue and vice were causal products like sugar and vitriol? It must be looked into, Berggrav believed, and so theology and philosophy remained the two most exciting areas of life. Here the solution must be found!

The practical conclusion was immediately clear. He must finish his theological studies and then must take up two minor subjects and become a teacher.

In the fall term he felt he must refuse the presidency of the Nordic Student Association. He did so without stating his real reason. He would not make an exhibition of his disbelief, just as later he would not make a show of his faith. However, he could not escape becoming a member of the Association's committee for a Nordic students' meeting in Finland. He was also elected leader of the trip. Norwegian speakers at the meeting included Ole Hallesby, Thv. Klaveness, and Chr. Bruun. Bruun gave an address on science and Christianity which hit the very center of Berggrav's problem. Yet, when the young man went rowing with Bruun, he could not bring himself to disclose his change of views to Bruun either.

He was venturesome enough in other ways. He did not hesitate to visit St. Petersburg (Leningrad) at a time when there was rioting and shooting in the streets. It was probably on this trip that he got the idea for his first best-selling book, *Soldiery and Religion*, written much later during the first World War while he was on a visit to Germany. He had found the answer to his questions about the truth of Christianity in a round-about way—in the fact that the human heart cannot do without it.

The only one young Berggrav talked to was Ole Iverson, later Dean Iverson. He said one thing that burnt itself into Berggrav's heart, "Whoever searches for the truth will always find it."

Actually he began the long way back that very summer of 1906. He threw himself into a study of the psychology of religion, with the Danish philosopher Harald Høffding as his master. He worked out a seminar paper for Professor Ording on the subject, "Motives for Religion." It was a forerunner of his doctor's dissertation and indicated a turn in the direction that was to lead him back to God.

The paper indicated also Berggrav's insight into what was to become the foremost problem of the future. On a trip to Marburg in the spring of 1907, he heard Professor Martin Rade speak on the relation between Christianity and modern science. Rade said, "We have the crisis of natural science behind us; we find ourselves now in the midst of the crisis of historical research; ahead we face our greatest problem—the clash between Christian faith and modern psychology."

In Norway this conflict did not reach a climax until 20 years later when it erupted in the debates on psychoanalysis in the 1920's. Then it was Berggrav who was able to come to the assistance of the young theologians. He had been through such struggles himself.

Berggrav's stay in Marburg turned out to be very significant for him. It had been advised and financed by his father, who had once spent a semester in Erlangen himself. "In our own country," his father said, "we have a narrow and bitter theology. You will have a broader horizon if you get around a little."

In Marburg Berggrav began a lifelong friendship with two important men—one was later to become Bishop Aulen, the other was Otto Holm-

dahl who was to become Director General. Berggrav was a faithful friend. He had friends in many
countries; and even years of separation did not
sever the ties which were strengthened by regular
correspondence. Aulen and Holmdahl came to Eivind Berggrav's funeral as representatives from
Sweden.

In Marburg Berggrav also met the Danish professor, Otto Ravn, who instilled in him a glowing
interest in the cause of South Jutland. On his way
home he visited South Jutland and saw with his
own eyes the German oppression there. He never
forgot it.

He was even bold enough to call on the famous
Harald Høffding at Copenhagen. They talked
frankly and intimately; and the younger man never
forgot Høffding's parting words: "The problems of
religion, my young friend, can never be wholly
solved. But life would not be worth living if the
questions were not there!"

Berggrav could always remember such words as
these, partly because of his unusually good memory
and partly because they expressed so clearly the
things that he himself felt. His own concepts were
sharpened in conversation with others.

Now, from time to time, he talked with others
about his spiritual problems. In Marburg he talked
with the foremost theologians, particularly with

Wilhelm Herman, who assured Berggrav that he would come through all right if he remained faithful to his religious experiences. Back home in Norway he talked with Erling Grønland, a pastor at Ullensaker. Grønland did not say much; he more or less listened. But Berggrav's words at Grønland's funeral many years later showed how infinitely grateful the younger man was for Grønland's gentleness and human warmth.

Berggrav's state examination in the fall of 1908 could fill a chapter by itself. His was probably the best class that ever graduated from the Theological School. The top scholars were Kolsrud, Mowinckel, and Hans Ording (all to become professors); two future rectors, Sten Bugge and Peter Marstrander; and Berggrav himself, who had had lower grades than any of the other honor students. He had written brilliantly in systematics, but his grades were lowered because he was not very good in the classical languages, Hebrew and Greek. So he barely made his *cum laude*. He had studied more philosophy and psychology than historical theology. History of theology had not been Otto Jensen's best subject either.

In the midst of these activities, light began to dawn for him and his faith. First came the direct question: "Why do I believe at all? Why aren't the materialists right?" The answer that came to him was that human life without spirit is weak and impoverished. Man is bankrupt if there is nothing more to life than the human body and the laws that govern it. He perceived that spirit is an independent reality not to be restricted by the laws of nature. He had learned that from Høffding. And through his observation of the characteristics of the spiritual world—its orderliness, its demands and ideals, which are common to everyone—he came to know God. In a letter to a friend he wrote, "Within our sphere of observation I consider the spirit the greatest reality, and within the spiritual world the greatest reality is the recognition of sin." On these two stones he built his house.

He came to see that man's need for God does not rise from fear or from wishful dreams. It is based, he believed, on what he later called man's "border-crossing" tendency. The human spirit is such that it continuously seeks to find what is on the other side of the border drawn by scientific facts. What lies beyond death? Where did existence spring from? To disregard such questions meant to Berggrav the renunciation of all human traits. Religion is therefore the deepest need of all, a necessity to all who are called human.

This realization led him to believe that God exists. The question of Christ was still a dilemma to him; but if God existed, then one could pray to

Him. Berggrav was not quick at beginning to pray again, nor had he ever entirely given up prayer. It is doubtful whether there was any long period in his life entirely without prayer. The fact that he could not help praying even when he did not "believe" must have been one reason for his not sliding farther away.

During the next few years there was a timid, quivering growth in his relation with God. Slowly belief was building up again, but he mistrusted every step that was not tested in the ordeal of doubt. Gradually he grew more confident. In the summer of 1910 he even served as an unordained chaplain with Nordland's battalion. He sensed a sort of awareness that the soldiers were doubters themselves and so might get something out of listening to someone like him. When anyone was actually helped, there was no limit to his joy. (See the article in *Kirke og Kultur* [Church and Culture], 1911, page 580.)

The person of Jesus attracted him. He rejected disdainfully the idea, popular at the time, that Jesus had probably never lived. That theory, he maintained, was contrary to the simplest historical facts. Besides, there was about Jesus something self-asserting. He was not an idea but a reality, a reality that outreached everything other men could give. Jesus Himself crossed over the border and was his-

torical fact. But for reasons connected with the
history of religion, Berggrav could not yet believe
that Jesus was truly the Son of God. The history of
religion had been too full of sons of gods. Besides,
the way to Jesus was made difficult by all theology,
by the varying "opinions" about Him.

Here, too, the crisis of 1906 became the turning
point for Berggrav on his way to the truth. The
emotional type of Christianity which had filled him
then was not whole and genuine; and the thought
struck him that it was Jesus who had let things
go as they did so that His kingdom should not
be spoiled by anything unnatural or untrue. This
thought helped free him from the many "opinions"
about a personal experience of Jesus. What finally
won him over completely was the intensity of Jesus.
"The closer I get to Him, the stronger He seems,"
he writes in one place.

The last big stumbling block was the Lord's Supper, which it seemed he could not accept because
of the many parallels found in the history of religion. Dr. Kristen Andersen helped him in this difficulty, especially by his articles in *Church and
Culture* and by a rich personal correspondence.

The Lord's Supper itself furnished the final solution. When Berggrav came to realize that Christ
was Christ, unique in Himself, and that He was, if
not the Son of God, nevertheless the one in whom

God *was* and *worked,* then he could refrain no longer from the sacrament. For Christ Himself had said, "Do this in remembrance of me." Berggrav had to obey.

It is characteristic that it was an act of obedience that finally carried him through. Berggrav must have been thinking of this when he later told us students, "The problem of doubt cannot be solved, only dissolved." It was a Christian action that won him completely.

In 1917, after eleven long years of doubt, he went again to communion. Nobody was to know about it. He went in to Oslo, to a church where he thought no one would know him. It was Vaterland Church, where he had once served as a Sunday school teacher. He tells us about it himself:

"Once upon a time there was a queer fellow in Northern Norway who asked me if there was any place for humor with the divine. To that I can answer yes, especially after what happened to me when I crept forward, trusting that no one would recognize me. As I took my place among the other communicants around the altar rail, my neighbor on my right was Peter Marstrander, and the one on my left was Hans Ording!"

The experience was a milestone, and his slow progress toward it was rewarded by the fact that there was no unhappy reaction. "And if you want

to have a picture of what gratitude is," Berggrav
wrote in a letter, "you should have photographed
the inside of me that Sunday afternoon."

The whole maturing process had been a gradual
resolving of the tensions within him. All the senti-
ments, thoughts, discussions, and experiences had
unconsciously united into something organic within him, so that he did not sense his faith until it
had become a reality. Thus it seemed clear to him
that faith is neither thought, nor emotions, nor in-
tellect, nor sentiment, but activity—a *function*
within the soul, accomplished not by oneself but
by God.

The rest of the road to his ministry has already
been told. It was his father who helped him get the
keystone in place.

To be sure, it was not all over. Berggrav bore the
marks of his experience for the rest of his life. A
positive influence appears in the fact that in Norway he was thereafter the pastor to those who are
searching. Negatively, he realized that he was often
too cautious and hesitant about direct evangelistic
work. If any one of us replied that it was good that
some were cautious since in our country we always
have plenty of eager soul-winners, he would shake
his head a little and say that nevertheless his way
was not quite what it should be.

He could never get over the fact that he himself had doubted so long, and that the eager ones could not help him then. He, therefore, was never one to try to push others into faith.

He drew them—slowly.

Chapter Four

The Woman
at His Side

ONE is tempted here to refer to the quotation, "He was very strong; there were women behind him." But in Berggrav's life there was only one woman—Kathrine Seip. Kathrine was the one who made him strong.

"The best thing about me is Kathrine," he used to say; and we did not contradict him for we knew that she was the best of all that he had.

Most people believed that they were direct opposites and that that was the reason they were attracted to each other. But it was not quite that way. To be sure they were quite different in the "tuning" of their personalities. He was fast and quick and full of wiles; she was slow, direct, and possessed of a good many of the inhibitions he lacked. But they operated on the same wave length with a sensitivity that was equally great in both. Perceptiveness in feeling, ability to take impressions and fix them in the memory, good judgment—all this they had in common. And both were shy. But whereas he covered up his reticence with a show of humor, she was cautious and painstaking in all her ways.

Their acquaintance began in the Christian Student Association. They met for the first time at an outing at Asker, although Berggrav later could not remember anything about that meeting. And he had little patience with people who talked about love at first sight.

It was on the long trip abroad in 1905 that they became friends. That was when Berggrav really discovered Kathrine. She had probably been, for once, a little ahead of him. For two whole years they were merely friends. A more sound basis for marriage is hard to find.

They had all kinds of interests in common. Both worked on the side as journalists. Kathrine was writing for the *Vestland Paper* and Eivind for the *Morning Paper*. They read a lot of Danish literature together, for Kathrine had attended a folk high school, where Grundtvigianism* had opened a new world to her. And at the University both were

---

*Grundtvig, Nikolai Frederik Severin (1783-1872), writer and educator, was the founder of the Danish folk high school.

members of a small clique that the Association
called "the family."

Kathrine at first studied science, but when the
curriculum was changed, she switched to philology.
She was an active Christian and thought of becoming a missionary. Both were open to the questions
of the times. They went to the theater and to meetings of the Students' Union, and got into the habit
of talking together about all that interested them.

One thing that brought them closer together was
the fact that Eivind had dared to tell her about
some of his spiritual problems and had met with
sympathetic understanding. This was more than
two years after they had got acquainted and a full
year after his great crisis. Their attachment grew
more slowly than is the custom now—and more
soundly!

In the fall of 1907 they became engaged in a
rather round-about way. Berggrav did not for the
life of him dare to ask Kathrine directly, for fear
of losing her as a friend if she would not have him
as a husband. And so he confided his hopes to Kathrine's closest friend, Ragna. At the news Ragna
threw her arms around his neck for sheer joy. Kathrine had confided in her just a short time before!
And so it was settled. They made no secret of their
indirect courtship, which remained a source of
much amusement to them and their friends.

During the next year they did not see very much of each other, since Eivind was studying in Germany from March until August and Kathrine went to Cambridge in October. For his birthday on October 25, he received three poems from her, one in Norwegian, one in English, and one in Latin. We have a few letters from that period which show a characteristic relationship between them—personal, straightforward, and concerned with reflections on and discussions of the problems of the times.

Prospects for an early marriage did not seem too bright. By Christmas of 1908 Berggrav was a graduate in Theology, but he still felt he could not become a minister and it was not easy for him to find other employment.

Then in the new year each of them, independent of the other, received an appointment to teach in the new People's High School at Eidsvoll. Berggrav had been sent to the school by his paper to cover the dedication ceremony in January. The principal, Jon Sørensen, told him that a certain Kathrine Seip had applied for a teaching position and had been accepted. Eivind asked at once if they would not take him too. They did. Kathrine was to teach Norwegian and arithmetic and to get 1,000 kroner a year; Eivind was to teach physics, chemistry and woodworking for 600 kroner. The spring and summer of 1909 were spent in preparation for teaching in the fall. He took a chemistry course in Oslo and a course in woodworking at Molde. Their wedding was celebrated on August 17 of that year.

Berggrav's father had been worried about the financial side of the venture, but all went well. Berggrav's pride knew no bounds when at the end of their first year together he could show a bank-book with savings amounting to 1,000 kroner. Of course he had been working as a journalist all year in addition to his teaching.

So it was that they established the home that was to become the center of Berggrav's life. It also became a shrine to their four sons and a source of heart-warming memories to the innumerable guests that were to visit it through the years.

To Berggrav himself the home was literally a shrine. He believed family life to be God's best gift to man and also the clearest revelation to us of what we have been created for. Marriage, he maintained, was vitalized by the very nerve of one's relationship to God; and something of God was realized in human love. In fact, one could almost say that in marriage love becomes flesh and dwells among us. Such was marriage between these two. And so it was that they could carry each other through the deep vicissitudes of life.

Kathrine was the stabilizer and critic. A basic trait was a warm, sincere honesty. She was exactingly truthful. She would not let any friendship develop unless she was sure that it would keep. She had a relationship with God so personal and self-sustaining that she influenced her husband's religious growth. When he looked back on the slow growth of his own faith, he said, half jokingly, "It is strange, but I am sometimes in doubt as to whether it was Kathrine or our Lord who was responsible for my progress." She would never have approved of such a statement! She became his counselor, not by giving advice, but by being what she was. Berggrav said once that she was "like an altar in the home."

He listened to his wife's counsel in all matters and advised other husbands to follow the same practice. She read his books and articles before anyone else was allowed to see them, and she sometimes had quite a job "bringing him back to earth." How often it happened, he once exclaimed, that Kathrine took the "best" points out of an article so that it went to the mailbox like a loaf of raisin bread without any raisins! But he hastened to add that it always came out that she had been right and that there were plenty of raisins left.

One time at a pastors' conference at Karasjok, Berggrav was suddenly taken sick just two hours

before he was to deliver the main address of the
meeting. His subject concerned intimacy and
alienation in friendship and marriage, as well as
other matters of mental health.* Great was the
disappointment of the ministers and their wives,
who had looked forward eagerly to hearing their
new bishop. Then, to their surprise, Mrs. Berggrav took over. "I shall try to present to you what
my husband would have said," she began. And then,
without any manuscript, she held her audience spellbound for an hour and a half. Some of those who
were there called it the best address they had ever
heard. "We'll get to hear Berggrav later," they said
afterwards, "but you should have heard Kathrine!"

The incident illustrates her ability to identify herself with her husband. She knew him inside and out,
understood his way of thinking, and watched his
changing moods. She admired him, she criticized
him, but she also knew that he had to be free to do
what he must. She did not interfere with his great
decisions, nor with his official duties. Her husband
was never one of those who have to ask their wives
first before making any decision. When she was
asked for advice, she spoke up frankly; and through
the years she had first place among all those to
whom Berggrav went for counsel.

In wartime she was indomitable. In 1942 she

---

*Berggrav's address was published later in his book, *Humor and Gravity*.

suffered a fall and a concussion of the brain. While
she was recovering she applied for permission to be
interned with her husband in the cottage at Asker.
The request was refused, and thereafter she maintained contact with Eivind by any means possible.
Those who met her at the West Railroad Station
during those years will not forget her. She would
come lugging the supplies that were to go out to
Berggrav—Swedish newspapers, forbidden newspapers, secret reports, and private letters cramming
her bag, and on top of it all a home-made cake as
camouflage.

The home she made for her family was a place all
its own. Someone once asked Berggrav what kind
of pastor's wife a man should choose, a woman who
could share her husband's interest and assist in the
parish, or one who would be a good homemaker and
housekeeper. He did not hesitate. "Choose the
homemaker," he said. He himself did not have to
make such a choice; he had his cake and ate it too.
Kathrine was both. She lived according to Bishop
Monrad's belief that "the pastor's wife has a share
in his calling for she is the one to help him, comfort
him, encourage him, and make him happy."

Berggrav, for his part, was a home-loving man.
Early in his career he wrote a short article, "Busy
at Home," in which he made the point that it is
quite permissible for one to refuse a request or in-

vitation on the grounds that one had set that day aside to be at home. An evening around the fireplace at Berggrav's house was like a party, both for the children and for all those who were included in their fellowship. The family revered their own special traditions, but were also alert and alive to new interests.

On April 7, 1949, Kathrine Berggrav died suddenly and quietly, just as she had wanted death to come. Berggrav felt as if he had undergone an amputation. He had shared every experience of mind and soul with Kathrine. In his grief he found that the Lord's Supper helped him. It seemed as if from his side of the Lord's table in the church he saw Kathrine within the circle on the other side. Moreover, she continued to live in his mind. He always knew what she would have said or advised, and he acted accordingly. It was a kind of fulfilment of her spirit within him.

It was true—Kathrine as well as his father had been a central person in his life. "She helped direct in me those things my father could not handle," he wrote in his bishop's *Vita*. It was a source of grateful joy to him that the two most important persons in his life enjoyed each other. Otto Jensen had become Dean of Oslo when his son was married, and he made many more trips up to Eidsvoll than he felt he should. But he enjoyed them!

Both father and wife were different from Berg-grav, but in much the same way. Each was firm as a rock, and they found each other in their devotion to Eivind's vibrant, exuberant being.

Berggrav realized what he owed them both. They were the solid rock beneath his feet, the stone that polished him. They furnished the firm foothold for his whole life.

Chapter Five

The Journalist

ALL his life Berggrav was a journalist both by temperament and by profession. From 1912 when he wrote his first article at the age of 18 until Christmastime in 1958 when he sent his last Christmas meditations to the *Hamar County News,* the *Agder Post,* and the *Hurdal Parish Paper,* Berggrav's articles were to be found regularly in newspapers and magazines.

Foremost among the periodicals he worked with was the magazine, *Church and Culture,* which he edited for fifty years, beginning in January 1909. The only interruptions in this long period of service were from 1922-1925 when Jens Gleditsch was the editor, and the war years from 1942-1945 when its publication was banned.

It was remarkable that Berggrav was entrusted

with the editorship of the magazine when he was
still so young. Who today would venture to give
such a responsibility to a 24-year-old graduate of
theology? It was Klaveness who did it then. He
and Christopher Bruun had started the periodical
in 1894. Bruun was now old, and Klaveness thought
the publication needed new blood. He himself
would stay on as associate editor.

It is hard to see how Klaveness dared to take the
step. *Church and Culture* was a part of his life, and
it had a definite program; its purpose was to build
a bridge across the widening gap between Christianity and modern culture. Two things must be
accomplished: the church itself must adopt a broad
outlook and become a church of the people, open to
everyone; and modern culture must be re-Chris-
tianized, else it would collapse in decay. The periodical became the strongest spokesman for Grundtvigianism in Norway, keeping in close touch at all
times with Danish intellectualism.

Klaveness was willing to put *Church and Culture*
into the hands of young Berggrav not only because
of a spark of daring in his own nature, but also
because Berggrav had already built up a considerable reputation as a journalist. His first article in
the *Stavanger Evening Paper* had pleased Klaveness, and Berggrav had later had some hard school-
ing in journalism under editor Nils Vogt of the

Morning Paper. Eivind had worked for the paper
as a free lance writer, searching for anything and
everything that he could turn into news. While he
was still in school, his writing became a steady
source of extra income. And all the time he was
learning about newspaper work. Vogt was sharply
critical. Berggrav's copy was frequently returned
to him embellished by the blue pencil lines and juicy
comments of his editor. But he was learning his
ABC's in the trade—how to report news. Reporting
was highly thought of; and woe to the journalist
whose reports were not reliable! The highest reward
a reporter could win was the approval of a person
whose speech he had covered. Such an honor came
to Berggrav once, when Bjørnstjerne Bjørnson himself called one morning and asked, "Who in the
world wrote this wonderful report?" Then Vogt,
bursting with editorial pride, embraced young
Berggrav. Some years later Berggrav's reports of
Harnack's addresses were published in book form.
Eventually he was also assigned to writing editorials.
In fact he was at one time almost at the point of
making journalism his full-time career. He hesitated
to do so, partly because editor Vogt warned him
about the hard life of a journalist, and partly because his father was opposed to it.

While he was considering the matter, the call to
teach in the high school at Eidsvoll had come as a

temporary solution to his problems. But Berggrav
always had a special place in his heart for journalists, as may be seen from his tribute to them in the
paper at *Tromsø:*

Journalists—they are the ones who dish up harsh comments
at will about the rest of us, without allowing us to say a single
word in reply—unless they want us to.

Journalists—they are the ones who can ask the rest of us
whatever they want to, and we have to answer—or else they
will say in the paper that we won't—but we can't ask them
anything at all.

Journalists—they are the ones who know more about us than
we do ourselves, although no one gets to know anything about
them.

Journalists—they are exciting people, more exciting than
firemen and aviators, for they are at the same time far-reaching
binoculars taking in events in the most distant parts of the
world, or special magnifying glasses making our own annual
meetings look like world events.

Journalists—they are at the same time party-throwers and
garbage men. They shave us when we need it and they trim
us up on anniversary days. They are wonders of versatility,
covering fish prices in Barcelona or weddings in Tromsø.
They provide sunshine for new ideas or poison spray for the
weeds of society. They are as light as radio waves or heavy
as Thor's hammer, as need may be.

In short, journalists share all our bad qualities and also all
the good ones we ourselves would like to have; so we are
furious when they use the bad ones and envious when they
use the good ones. And never do we thank them!

The comment shows his understanding of the
difficult profession of the journalist; it reflects his
affection for his former colleagues; and it has a

twinkle of irony in its subtle self-portraiture. It is in itself a journalistic gem.

Berggrav reached his height as a writer in his book, *Land of Suspense*. In it he shows his ability to capture mood and feeling, his keen perceptiveness of detail, and his art of bringing the whole alive to the mind of the reader. He did not think highly of his own "scribblings." He called his books mummies, standing there dead on the shelves. There was one exception; he liked the chapter on Makkaur, the rock island off the Varanger peninsula with its 102 inhabitants who nonetheless managed to raise a church of their own. It is an unforgettable essay, and through reprints in anthologies of literature it has become known to nearly every child in Norway.

Berggrav has been noted for his ability to coin expressions that strike home, both in writing and speaking. At times his figures of speech may seem far-fetched, as if he strained to put a Berggrav stamp upon everything he said. But what he was always trying to do was to hit the target linguistically and at the same time to hit the hearts of his hearers—to rouse them by saying things in an unusual or striking way.

Once in a while, of course, he happened to be unfortunate in his wording, as when in an article about the lepers of Madagascar written for *Church and Culture* he chose the title "The Lepers Beckon"

("De spedalske lokker"). We can be sure his wife
was not around when he sent that in.

But many of his expressions are out-and-out
clever. They pop up in his remarks or as titles of
books or chapter headings. During the war Berggrav was asked to write an account of the situation
in Norway when it was extremely serious. He began
the article with the statement, "The main issue
about any situation is that it should not be the
main issue."

His most influential period as editor of *Church
and Culture* was probably from 1925 to 1937,
when he became Bishop of Oslo. One discovers at
this time an increasing warmth in his style, with
an emphasis on spiritual concern which helped
many in their attempts to have a deeper Christian
faith. He used all of his psychological skill to help
people find Christ. "Obedient to the Faith" and
"The Doubter's Place in the Church" are characteristic titles from these years. The journalist had
become a pastoral counselor without losing any
of his freshness in the process.

Berggrav possessed that special sense which is indispensable to journalists—the sense of knowing be-
forehand what will be timely. He had a talent for
publishing a thing at the right moment. There was,
for example, the pamphlet *Contra Castberg* which
was available right after the Church Department

had published Professor Castberg's opinion on the
legal status of the church in relation to the state.

His foresight also appears in an article in *Church
and Culture,* April 1911, "What Withers and What
Grows." It was an "attack on ourselves" and on the
barren doubts of the theologians who could only
strip away the withered leaves of the old dogmas
without taking note of the "new romanticism" that
was emerging. In the article Berggrav wrote,

> We can mark the changes of time by looking at a statement
> Brandes made in about 1880, "All spiritual science is natural
> science." Today the proposition can be turned around and
> we can say, "Natural science itself has proved to be spiritual
> science." It is a complete revolution.

The revolution did not become apparent to most
others until long afterward, although Gerhard
Gran's book *Religious Unrest* pointed in the same
direction. But Berggrav was one of the first churchmen to recognize that we were facing a time of
uprising for the church, that our best days lay ahead
of us, not behind. The truth did not become apparent to most of us until the great revival movements
of the 1930's. But Berggrav had sensed it first.

In 1928, when he wrote his famous conciliatory
article about liberal theology, labeling it the "theology of an era," he was only expressing again what
he had been saying and writing for a long time.
That school of theology had been a necessary phase

of transition. At the same time it was a vigorous "Christian reducing treatment." Now the "fires were burning and new thoughts and opinions were in the making."

As a journalist he had been able to mark the changing times. As a scientist he had been testing them. As an educator he was prepared to face them.

Chapter Six

The Educator

BERGGRAV said that his ten years in teaching, from 1909 to 1919, seemed to have had no noticeable influence upon others. The first five years he taught at Eidsvoll in the folk high school. In 1914-1915 he was substitute principal at the teacher's college at Holmestrand. From 1915 to 1919 he was principal of the county school at Nerdrum in Fetsund. Berggrav saw something symbolic in the fact that not one of these schools still exists. The first two were closed, and the third was moved to Jessheim. His teaching career amounted to some broken pieces—a few short years in each place, until he became a pastor at Hurdal in 1919.

Nonetheless, these years were of great importance to Berggrav himself.

First of all, they brought him back to rural Nor-

way. During his boyhood he had lived in the country until he finished the Middle School, and his
love of the country took root at that time. Then he
had lived in the city, first in Stavanger and later
in Oslo. He became well acquainted with Europe,
especially with Germany, but he did not really
know rural Norway until he went to Eidsvoll. At
that time he was marked by a kind of urban-provin-
cialism typical of many Oslo-reared people who
have seen little of country life.

But the high school opened up a new world to
him—one populated by the young folks from the
Østland farms. Here he met his own childhood
again, and the country boy from Asak achieved his
confirmation. Now he read Chr. Bruun's *Basic
Ideas of the People (Folkelige Grunntanker)* and a
great deal of literature about the Danish folk high
schools, and he believed that he had found his life
work—he was to be a teacher in the youth schools.
Meanwhile he traveled all through the Østland section giving lectures, especially in the academies. He
also made two long lecture tours into North Norway, establishing a number of folk academies there.
His simplicity of manner and ability to reach people
of all sorts perhaps stemmed from this period.

Moreover, Berggrav had benefited greatly from
his actual teaching. In the first years he had taught
primarily chemistry and woodwork, with some

arithmetic. He was also house-master at the boys' dormitory. Later he taught history and worked hard to master the subject himself. When Erling Grønland left, Eivind became the theologian of the school and taught psychology.

The folk-school movement was characterized by its opposition to the emphasis of the regular schools on memorization and "cramming." It has done the Norwegian schools a tremendous service because so many of its teachers came from folk high schools where they had discovered the importance of learning drawn from living, spoken words. Here the chief objective was direct contact with the pupils. It was the pupil's personality that was to be developed, and students were to work with a subject in such a way that it would seem alive and significant to them. Then they would understand it themselves, and memorization would be unnecessary.

This sort of teaching was precisely suited to Berggrav's lively, friendly nature, and it undoubtedly helped develop his easy manner at desk or rostrum.

During this period, Berggrav met all sorts of teachers, and these contacts helped him in his work with the schools after he became bishop. Because he knew the problems of the teachers from his own experience, he could meet the instructors on his formal visitations or at teachers' meetings more like one of them than like an official visitor. Folks still talk about a teachers' course he held in the winter of 1937-38, soon after he became Bishop of Oslo. And phrases from his lectures at that time are still quoted in the teachers' rooms in the various grade schools. His talks helped many teachers to formulate excellent courses of religious instruction for the schools. Berggrav always emphasized the fact that the child himself must be the center of any program of learning. The child was not only someone that the school was preparing to become a man, he was a person already and a part of the stream of humanity. Therefore no pupil is to be taught according to what he should be as an adult, but rather according to what he already is as a child.

Berggrav proclaimed these ideas, so typical of the folk high school movement, during his years as a teacher. And later he set them down in the small but momentous book, *Religion and the Soul of the Child* (1949).

One reason that Berggrav did not remain an educator in the folk school may be found in the rising controversy about the Norwegian language. The folk schools took sides with the New (or vernacular) Norwegian; and although Berggrav was an advocate of the popular language, he thought that the New Norwegian was too strongly shaped according to the Vestland (Western Norway) dialect.

And then a conflict arose among some of the leaders
of the folk schools. Berggrav had had plans for
establishing a "top school" similar to the one at
Askov in Denmark. The plans were almost finished,
and he had secured as co-workers his brother-in-
law, Didrik Arup Seip, and a former schoolmate
from Stavanger, Olaf Devik. The school was to
include a graduate school for teachers. One of the
things Berggrav was promoting was a greater concentration of learning in the educational system.
He proposed fewer courses, with greater emphasis
on one major subject.

Then the whole plan collapsed at the annual
meeting of the Folk High School Teachers' Association. Berggrav could not and would not promise
to speak the New Norwegian. He was too much of
an East Norwegian for that. And he did not want
to set up the school with such controversies arising
at the very beginning.

Instead, with Didrik Seip, who was an expert
in philology, he started a movement that for some
time seemed significant but is now almost forgotten. Berggrav with his talent for titles called it
the "Østland Revolt." It had a two-fold purpose:
first, it was opposed to the strong Western influence in the New Norwegian language; and second, it was opposed to the strong Danish influence
in the Official Norwegian (the Riksmål). Eastern

Norway had been caught napping, Berggrav thought; now it must be aroused. Eastern Norway had let the language reform slip into the hands of people favorable to the Telemark and West Norway dialects; and, so far as their own feelings were concerned, they had yielded to the official language of the Eastern cities. Now, however, they should dare to use their own Eastern vernacular.

Seip and Berggrav received unexpected support from Halvdan Koht, who was known as a New-Norwegian man. Berggrav was to be promoter and publicity man as well as the chairman of the Østland Revolt. Koht became vice-chairman, while Seip and Torgeir Krogsrud attacked the philological problems. Their plan was to allow Østland children to use their own language for written work in school. Thus the term "optional forms" came into use. For example, it would be allowable for Østland children to use the word "kua" (a popular form for *cow*), something that was not "nice" in the spoken language and that was not used at all in the official written Norwegian.

But the whole movement collapsed when a cabinet member named Løvland—a New-Norwegian man—took up the matter and wanted to make the optional forms compulsory. And so it happened that what was to have been accomplished naturally and freely, came about as a dictate from one *Lands-mål* (New Norwegian) man. Seip and Berggrav were in despair. Many stormy meetings were held in all parts of Østland, and hundreds of letters of protest against the vulgarization of the language held Berggrav responsible for promoting it.

For Berggrav it was a real fight. For the first time he became the main target of attack. He even had to stop speaking in the middle of an address at a school district meeting because the member of the board in charge of the use of the building refused to let him continue. Berggrav had to leave the meeting, and the board member took over.

The Østland Revolt did not die out until 1922. The cause had been taken over by politicians and never became a movement of the people, as Berggrav had hoped it would. So it just died out. But in the spelling reform of 1938, it may be said to have come to life again. The new orthography included practically all the forms that Berggrav and his associates had proposed. Only they had hoped that the changes would come about voluntarily instead of by decree.

Berggrav's year at Holmestrand came about almost accidentally. After resigning from Eidsvoll, he was without a job. The war had broken out in 1914 and things looked gloomy. Then he was appointed substitute principal for one year at the teachers' college in Holmestrand. He was very happy there. He taught the *Landsmål,* or "country language," and learned to speak and write the new language. Berggrav was still considered such a liberal in religion that he taught no courses in Christianity at this school, nor was he even allowed to speak on religious issues outside school hours.

The next summer, when Berggrav was about to apply for the position of permanent principal at the teachers' college, he was urged to apply instead for the principalship of the new County School at Fetsund. "Køla-Pålsen's" farm at Nerdrum had been bought for the school. The County Board accepted his application, and in the fall of 1915 Berggrav found himself busy with preparations for the opening of the new school. He suggested the addition of a new shop subject—metal work—and headed a drive to raise funds for remodeling the old hog house into a shop for carpentry and blacksmithing. There was an excellent spirit of cooperation among the young teachers of the school; and the years at Fetsund were full of life and fun.

Great emphasis was put upon cooperating with the community. Garden parties in the summer and meetings in the school gymnasium in the winter drew large numbers to the school. In those days of food shortages, Berggrav became chairman of the Board of Provisions and of the Board of Controls

over farm products. He measured the grain bins on
the farms, distributed pig-subsidies to small farm-
ers, and lectured on potato raising so eloquently that
people "wept for potatoes," as an old friend, Ole
Aanesen, expressed it. More and more Berggrav became bound up with Akerhus county life. He
familiarized himself with local history and with
county economy and county politics. But he stayed
out of party politics.

He naturally had plans for developing Nerdrum
into a large school. Typhoid fever put a stop to his
plans. Every year there was typhoid in Fetsund.
Parents feared to send their children to the school;
and when several deaths occurred in the community
one year, Berggrav knew that the fate of the school
had been settled. He suggested that it be moved to
Sørumsand. At the same time he was appointed
chairman of the planning committee for a new
modern school at Nordby Lake near Jessheim. He
intended to move to Jessheim, and Norway's best
equipped young people's school was later built there.
But by that time Berggrav was out of the school
picture. The school teacher had become a man of
the church.

However, he never forgot the schools, and in his
later life he did a great deal of work with school
problems in addition to his duties as official visitor.
We should mention especially his two Christian

textbooks, a Bible history and an edition of Luther's
Catechism with exercises. In the latter Berggrav
dealt with the difficult question of the text itself.
Luther had published two editions of the Catechism; and he had been quite free in his translations
of such passages from the Bible as the Ten Commandments. Berggrav had explained all this in his
Revision of the Catechism (1936), a forerunner of
his own edition of the Catechism.

At one point Berggrav did something entirely
different. When the Church Department passed
upon the final text of the Catechism, it accepted
Berggrav's wording of the eighth commandment.
The Bible itself and Luther used the wording,
"Thou shalt not bear false witness against thy
neighbor." And Berggrav used it, too, in his original
version. But in his Catechism he took a short-cut;
keeping in mind effective teaching principles,
he used the wording, "Thou shalt not lie." And that
is the way all the children learn it today. It is a
departure from the letter and tradition of the Bible,
but anyone must agree with Harald Aspås's comment *(Luther's Catechism as a Text Today,* page
59): "It is clever, and right to the point. It hits
what is surely the most common sin of children—
lying. This wording of the commandment will make
a clear impression on the mind of any child, whereas in its original form it has no meaning at all to

young children and is intelligible to older ones only
after considerable explanation."

The revision is typical of Berggrav; it is daring
but fundamental, and it is actually in close accordance with the true intention of the commandment.

The exercises in Berggrav's Catechism are short
and clear, but they pre-suppose much work on the
part of the teacher. They indicate Berggrav's faith
in the teachers of Norway; they do not need elabo-
rate directions but only brief pointers indicating
how each teacher can give his or her own explana-
tions to the children orally. Another innovation in
Berggrav's Catechism is his inclusion of Luther's
chapter on the confession, which had hitherto been
omitted from the Norwegian school editions.

Actually Berggrav's career as an educator com-
prises much more than his ten years in the classroom; it was a part of him for the rest of his life.
Like his father, he was a born teacher. For him the
essential element in teaching was the contact between teacher and pupil. He always wanted to say
things so that they would be understood, even by
children, and he wanted always to sense a vital contact between himself and those who heard him.

He was an exceptionally good minister to children and a good catechist in the church. It was not
easy for him. His psychological type of sermon was

not in line with a child's thinking; but he was superbly effective in the midst of a throng of children on his visits to the schools. This success he undoubtedly owed, at least in part, to his years as a classroom teacher.

Chapter Seven

The Scholar

A SCHOLARLY dissertation is usually not entertaining reading. It is not meant to be. Humor would only destroy the serious tone that such books ought to have

And so Berggrav felt himself somewhat handicapped as a scholar. He could never learn to be dull. He loathed dullness; he had to say things in fresh, new ways. During the 20's when he was trying to prepare himself for a professorship, there were many who looked upon his scholarly papers as if they were just the work of a journalist.

Yet this was the period when Berggrav made his greatest contribution to the student world. In the spring of 1928 he was chairman of the Norwegian Students' Christian Association and was lecturing to packed audiences at the University. The students

looked upon him as something of a pioneer in spirit.
By this time the controversies over liberal theology
were over, and the present concern was for a great
new era for the whole Norwegian Church. This
transition period came about the time that Berggrav was appointed Bishop of Hålogaland in 1929.

We who began our studies in 1928 will never forget his lectures at the University. As recent college
graduates we scarcely had the background for them,
for psychology of religion—if included at all—came
much later in our course.

But Berggrav fascinated us at once. He put it all
on the blackboard for us: the connection between
body and soul; the conative, the cognitive, and the
emotional elements in the life of the soul, with God
the great Director over all. He helped us grasp the
meanings of the at first incomprehensible foreign
words; he was at home with the psychoanalytical
way of thinking and we tried to absorb it in every
pore. I have never in my life heard such fascinating
lectures as he gave us then.

He would also answer questions from the students, anonymous ones, sometimes of very intimate
nature. At times he would ask the unknown in-
quirer to come to see him privately. We had the
feeling that something was happening among the
students.

There was real sorrow among us when he was

appointed Bishop of Hålogaland in October of
1929. There were stirring speeches by the students
about the great loss to the University. But Berggrav took it calmly: "To tell the truth, gentlemen,
this subject has always been more a passion with me
than a science. Now I'm through with it!" It was
certainly true, as a German professor once told him,
that he pursued his studies passionately.

The whole background for his philosophical work
was deeply personal and was closely connected with
his period of doubt. The solution of his crisis came,
as we saw, with the help of psychology. He had discovered that, although the content of faith and
religion can be discussed, religion itself is an indis-
putable fact in the human soul. The more one
studies this fact, the clearer it becomes that the
motives for religion lie deeper within the soul than
many realize. Religion is not a rudiment from the
childhood of man—not something that with man's
increasing knowledge and progressing development
will fall away by itself. It is a primordial, natural
phenomenon in us, rooted in our very being.

It was at this time that Berggrav coined his
phrase, "the border-crossing tendency." The idea it
expressed had been the theme of his doctor's dissertation in 1925. He had entitled it, "The Threshold of Religion."

Perhaps the thought had its roots in a childhood

memory from his Asak days. In the lower end of the pasture there had been a waterfall about ten feet high. It was fun to play in the pool below the falls. Then once, while playing there, he was seized by an uncontrollable curiosity: Where did the little stream come from? He followed it across the field, past a farmhand's place, and way up into the woods. Finally he had to stop. But he had not found the answer to his question. He still did not know where the stream came from. He was then and he continued to be concerned about what lay beyond the border.

At least it is certain that in his doctor's thesis Berggrav began with a similar thought. At that time German philosophers were busily discussing the question of the differences between men and animals. So Berggrav tried to imagine a smart animal, like a horse for instance, inside a large enclosure with a high fence around it so that the animal could not see over it or through it. Inside the fence is everything that a horse could want—food, water, and plenty of room; and there are no sounds or smells from outside to attract the attention of the horse. Now if there is nothing to arouse the interest of the horse on the outside, it will not mind the fence at all or care about what is on the other side of it, not even when it is satisfied and rested.

But a human being under similar circumstances

would inevitably become interested in the fence or
wall. Wherever a man is stopped by a border, an
immediate interest is aroused in him concerning
the boundary and what lies beyond it. And this
border-crossing tendency, Berggrav believed, is fundamental in the nature of man.

In his works Berggrav analyzes this tendency in
the world of thought, in the will, in sensory perception; and he shows that religion has its own place
and its own threshold in man's consciousness. Religion is a particular experience to be found in "the
encounter between the outstretched hand of man
and an answering hand which one is peculiarly
aware of being clasped by, but which nonetheless
must be reached for." Berggrav discusses both the
mystic and the ecstatic views on the subject, but
his heart is really church-minded so that he empha-
sizes the experience in ordinary everyday Christian
life.

His doctor's disputation was not without its
dramatic moments. Professor Ragnar Vogt, M.D.,
was sharply opposed to Berggrav's views; and Kristian Schjelderup, TH.D., appeared as a special opponent, inspiring this headline in Paul Gjesdahl's
report for *Dagbladet* (Daily Paper): "Dr. Schjelderup Attempts to Trip Berggrav on the Threshold
of Religion."

Berggrav's optional trial lecture was on the place of fear in the religious life. In the first section, "Born in Fear?" he rejected the old conception that apprehension is the chief motive for religion. Then he tried to show the positive force of fear in religion, concluding with the text, "The fear of the Lord is the beginning of wisdom." The test lecture is by far one of the best things Berggrav ever wrote, and we agree with Vogt that it ought to have been the first chapter of his dissertation.*

As early as 1923 Berggrav had become an honorary doctor at the University of Lund. This school was his spiritual home, rather than the University of Oslo. He also spent considerable time at Copenhagen, where the great Edward Lehmann was his teacher. In 1915 Lehmann had rejected Berggrav's first draft for his dissertation, a paper he had half finished during his stay in England in 1914. Berggrav later said that this paper was so poor that he should have given up his scholarly pursuits then and there.

In 1915 he received an invitation from Germany to come to the front lines to study the psychology of war. For two months, in the interval between Holmestrand and Fetsund, he was in Germany, and

---

*Both the Dissertation and Vogt's opposition (with Berggrav's replies) appear in *Norsk Theologisk Tidsskrift (Periodical of Norwegian Theology)* 1926, No. 1.

not long afterward he wrote his first book, *Soldiery and Religion (Krigerliv og Religiøsitet)*, which bears witness to his psychological discernment. The book was very popular. There were two printings at once, as well as later reprints, and it was also translated into Swedish and Finnish.

Another little book from this period, *The Man Jesus* (1921), is a cautious psychological study of the person of Jesus, stressing especially His many traits. At the time, the book expressed some of Berggrav's innermost thoughts, but in later years he was dissatisfied with it and often thought of rewriting it under a new title, *The Man Jesus—Christ the Lord*. The change in title indicates what the first edition lacked.*

Shortly after Berggrav's doctor's dissertation, his second important book appeared, *Religious Feeling in the Healthy Soul* (1927). It is an answer to Cardinal Newman's harsh judgment of Protestantism to the effect that "Luther found men in slavery to their works, but he left them in slavery to their emotions."

Berggrav admits that the statement may be partly truth so far as modern Protestantism is concerned, but he proves that it is far from the truth

---

*The book was republished in 1941 with an addition about Jesus as the physician of the soul *(The Man Jesus—Physician of the Soul)*, but this reprint is not the book Berggrav dreamed of writing.

about Luther. He shows himself to be a great Luther scholar, and he brings a charge against that adulteration of Christianity which the modern emotional emphasis has become, in his opinion. Both theoretically and practically he makes it clear that religious feeling is only one accompanying feature, never the main feature, of Christian life. It is a symptom of disease when emotionalism is valued for itself; for if religious feeling becomes a source of enjoyment, it marks a dangerous sort of self-centeredness.

Berggrav never conceives of religion as an existence in a world of feelings. In this respect he differs from other theologians, like Rudolf Otto, whom he agreed with in other respects. Berggrav never conceives of religion as a part of one's psyche, but rather as an action of the spirit; and the feelings that accompany it are only incidental, without value in themselves.

And so in this book Berggrav pleads once more for the pious life of the ordinary man. It is healthy, natural, everyday phenomena that concern him, and the whole book is an expression of his affection for the Norwegian type of Christianity as most people practice it.

Berggrav's last philosophical book, *Body and Soul in Relation to Man's Character and Religion,* 1933, presents a departure from two earlier studies in this field. *Body and Soul* is based upon his work with experimental psychology.

Here Berggrav is dealing with that borderland which lies between medicine and psychology. His background for the study grew out of some studies in medicine and certain physiological experiments he had participated in at Lund University. In the book he anticipates some developments that were not generally recognized until after World War II, especially in the field of psychosomatic medicine. He also displays unusual insight into neurology, particularly with reference to the vegetative nervous system.

There was a personal background for his interest in the field. In his early forties Berggrav suffered from neurasthenia; he was overworked and became depressed and scarcely able to work at all. He sought help in many places, but without avail until he became interested in some of the new methods of relaxation. He could do the exercises perfectly and learned by experience how proper relaxation can improve one's state of mind. He did the exercises regularly. He also experimented with his diet, much to the regret of the pastors' wives who prided themselves on their cooking, for he began to eat as sparingly as possible.

His studies almost made him a somatologist; that

is, he allied himself with that school of thought which stresses the importance of the body *(soma=* the body) in relation to the mind, holding that the treatment of nervous diseases ought to begin by building up a healthy body and a well disciplined life. His knowledge in the field was comprehensive. In fact, one doctor said that Berggrav could set up a case history just as well as a psychiatrist could.

In his book on the body and the soul, Berggrav deals with the philosophical and theological questions raised by these studies: Are a person's mental state and all the ups-and-downs of his emotions only the reflections of his particular physiological reflexes? He comes to this conclusion: With God as Lord over both body and soul, with all things in His hand, He can play on all the strings.

The contents of the book were first presented as Olaus Petri Lectures at Uppsala University. They made such a sensation that three times the auditoriums had to be changed to accommodate the crowds. The last lectures were given in the Aula, and still there was not enough room.

"I do not remember that I ever before realized how completely a great personality can sway a crowd with his oratory," writes Sven Stolpe in his book, *Five Norwegians.* And he continues, "For long periods the audience would sit deathly silent, spellbound by his sparkling style, lost in wonder at

the new perspectives being opened before them.
Then would come laughter as this Norwegian
preacher would relate some homely anecdote or let
his friendly irony play."

*

How is one to judge Berggrav as a scholar?

He was very critical of himself. As we have said
before, neither Eivind nor his father considered
themselves real scholars. His intellectual endow-
ments were good enough, he thought, for side-line
activities; but he was not single-minded enough,
or not sharply decisive enough to carry through any
monumental scholastic achievement.

Was he right about that?

One thing is certain; for the present, at least,
time has passed him by. He was actually neither a
theologian nor a psychologist—at any rate not an
experimental psychologist—but moved on the bor-
derline, philosophizing between the two fields. But
just at this time a new trend in theology developed,
introduced primarily by Karl Barth. With increasing strength it has filtered into the theology of all
the churches. Its proponents had no interest in
psychology. They were concerned only with what
is objective: not with the human threshold of religion, but with God's revelation; not with religious
feeling, but with church doctrine; not with what
is religiously sound, but with what is true.

In a way Berggrav had a part in this reaction, just as he had reacted against the attempts of the Liberalists to "shave down" Christianity to a doubtful "nucleus." But Berggrav looked for the center of religion in the sound religious life of the soul; whereas Barth and his followers have found it in the revelation of the Bible.

Berggrav in this respect aligned himself with Rudolf Otto and Friedrich Heiler, the leading theologians during the 1920's after the culmination of the Liberals and before Barth had made a name for himself. Berggrav had helped to make these men known in Norway. They were preparing the ground for a new theology in the church, and Berggrav was doing the same thing here in Norway by resisting the "Christianity-reducing movement" and by urging a return to a fully mature Christian life.

Today as one reads Berggrav's books, one realizes that the present generation of theologians thinks differently. The language itself is different. We cannot say "religion" and "religious" with the connotations and feeling Berggrav gave them. To him they were concepts embracing all Christianity, whereas in more recent theology, religiosity and Christianity appear as alternative terms.

But if Berggrav represents the end of a period in theology and is therefore not significant as a scholar today, I have no doubt that posterity will see him in a different light. His works present so many original concepts and such keen, forward-looking ideas that they will have something to say to the theology of tomorrow. At present it seems that the psychology of religion attracts little attention, but it is certain to return to a position of importance. And then Berggrav's works will not be disregarded. His presentation of the deep connection between elemental human nature and the work of religion within the soul is a basic contribution to religious thought. His views about the relation between body and soul in man's character and religious experience have received too little attention, though it has been given new significance by modern psychiatry.

Finally, it is extremely significant that Berggrav has always confined his studies in the field to the *healthy* spiritual life. His interests were not with the great waves of emotional piety of the revivalists or the experiences of the mystics. He was too much of an East Norwegian for that. It is the simple, shy, religious life that concerns him, and in that field he remains the religious psychologist to the church at large.

One could write another chapter on Berggrav as a biographer. He has brought forth a long list of biographies of men of the church. Probably the most important of these works is the book *Profiles*

of the Norwegian Church. He did his final editing
of it during his internment in the cottage at Asker,
but the first three biographies—those of Christopher
Bruun, Thv. Klaveness, and J. J. Jansen—had been
written ten years earlier. The article on Bruun,
written for *Church and Culture* in 1926, was con-
siderably enlarged upon for the book. At the cottage he wrote up the lives of Gustav Jensen, Johs.
Johnson, and Erling Grønland. The book was published in 1946.

It is one of his finest works, historically accurate
yet perceptive and sympathetic. In it he unfolds his
learning and his individual talents—his historical
interests, his journalistic style, his fine perception
of detail, his psychological insights, and his broad
outlook over the whole church field. It is good reading. The characters come to life in it, and one has
the feeling that Berggrav was fond of each of them.

The strongest portrait is probably the one of
Christopher Bruun, in whom Berggrav had been
interested for years. Bruun had been the inspiration
for the principal character of Bjørnson's *Beyond
Our Power (Over Ævne)* and of Ibsen's *Brand.*
And so Berggrav became interested in Ibsen. Together with Francis Bull he presented the opposition
to Halvdan Wexelsen Freihow's doctor's treatise on
"Henrik Ibsen's *Brand.*" The comments of the two
opponents are to be found in the book *Ibsen's Spir-*

itual Crisis, 1937. Berggrav also wrote a literary exposition on *Christopher Bruun's Relation to Ibsen's "Brand."*

In his analysis of the Brand-image, Berggrav applied C. G. Jung's theory about psychological types. He takes the view that Ibsen belonged to the strongly introverted type of artist, thus throwing new light on Ibsen's "Brand crisis."

Among Berggrav's many other biographies, three are especially outstanding: one on Archbishop *Nathan Söderblom,* written shortly after Söderblom's death; and two little studies, on *Petter Dass, the Christian Singer,* and on *Elias Blix.* We should mention also his *Bishops' Gallery,* a reprint of articles written for th*e Morning Post.* The series includes biographical sketches of the bishops of Oslo from the time of the Reformation to the present. The earliest sketches are careful historical studies; the later ones display Berggrav's aptness at hasty characterizations. For example, he writes, "Bishop Bugge's style was academically fine-grained; Bishop Bang's was popularly coarse-grained."

One is tempted to turn the tables and ask, And what about Berggrav's style as a biographer and writer?

The answer is easy. His style is both ways. He could be minutely exact in the matter of details, and he employed the best scholarly techniques in finding and using source materials. He had folders of clippings, quotations, and information about persons and things he might some day want to write about. These details would grow within him until finally the full portrait would emerge. This he would sketch in swift, bold lines, fitting in the significant details and accenting the ones he felt most characteristic.

This same correlation between the details and the whole typifies Berggrav the scholar. He loved the great perspectives within the limits of a unifying viewpoint. But he did not neglect the details, even though they were consigned to a secondary place in the great sweep of his learning.

Chapter Eight

The Churchman

PASTOR, AFTER ALL!

THE death of his father in February 1918 had a tremendous impact on Berggrav. His old friend, Jon Sørensen, wrote in a letter of condolence, "When the big tree falls, the young tree's roots will loosen too." That is just the way Berggrav felt about it. "For my father," he wrote, "I feel no sorrow; for myself there is nothing but sorrow."

He felt, he said, as if he were walking through empty rooms in a house he was about to leave, knowing that he could never come back to live there any more. His old doubts brushed past him like cold, distant gusts; yet at the same time he felt strongly, "How wonderful is our Christian

faith against this Lilliputian world! How wonderful our knowing that the soul is above all death!"
In the midst of this tension, his most disturbing
uncertainty was probably concerned with whether
or not he would dare to become a minister.

Within a few months he was clear about that
matter. As we have seen, he made his decision at the
annual fall festival at the University that year. He
applied for and was accepted by the parish at Hurdal, the only community in Romerike which he had
not visited as a lecturer. He did not enter his pastorate until the end of the school year in May, 1919,
so he had plenty of time for thinking during the
winter.

The appointment to Hurdal was the keystone
marking the completion of a slow, maturing process. In spirit he had become a pastor before he applied for a parish. The death of his father simply
released the tension. What had already unfolded
within him was now complete. It had become reality. He knew now that he would live and die in the
faith, even if the whole world were to contradict
him. Pouring the foundation had taken time, but
slow hardening makes the best concrete. The pressure of life itself had determined the direction of
his life.

In a letter to a friend about a month after his

appointment, he looked back over the long road leading to his call to the ministry.* In this letter he also explained the kind of preaching he intended to do:

I don't think I will ever be the aggressive type of minister. I do not feel like "breaking in" on people. I do wish to gather in all who come with a deep, heartfelt yearning. Those are the ones I want to meet in church. And so I do not have any outside ambitions for my work. I may not even make a good pastor. I cannot go about it in any other way than my "call" leads me.

This remained the program for his whole life as a churchman, from his first service at Hurdal to his last one in the Oslo Cathedral on January 20, 1959. He wanted to be pastor to the weak ones, the longing ones. His concern was for the tender sprouts. He could be hasty or quick-spoken with the confident, self-satisfied type. But with the real doubter, the trembling heart, he became soft as wax.

He could be critical of the Oxford Movement or of the Inner Mission or of other revivalistic movements with their overconfident approach, and he could use strong words against them. But if such a worker talked with him personally, he melted at once. Many are the Oxford leaders and

---

*It was always easier for Berggrav to write personally than to talk personally about the deepest experiences of life. He needed a certain distance when he was discussing intimate problems. His shyness required it. The same thing was true with both friends and family. He was old-fashioned about it. Today people hardly ever have time to write such letters.

Inner Mission men who had this experience with Berggrav. He reacted strongly against any sort of arbitrary lines drawn or any prejudicial position taken in Christian work. But if he could get behind the lines and see into the heart of the work, he found himself completely in tune with it. In reality he was related to the revivalists. Their common ground was their emphasis on personal contact. He was afraid that the young leaders of the Neo-orthodox group, in their zealous rediscovery of doctrine and liturgy, might overlook this personal touch. He despaired if one of us ever gave a purely doctrinal sermon. Then we would be called in for an interview. It was the heart of the matter that counted. He would listen for the sound of this deeply personal touch—that we all knew. And when he heard its tones, all criticism melted away. He had a radar-like sense when it came to feeling the true relationship between a man and God. Although he hesitated to come right out and say so, it was always this that he was looking for.

This sense of the personal touch was characteristic of all his work in the church—as pastor, as bishop, as organizer, and as ecumenical leader.

It was in evidence at Hurdal, where he began as just an ordinary Norwegian pastor. His position had been pictured to him by Dr. Kristen Anderson, who had encouraged him to become a minister:

"God is now going to take you away from the wholesale kind of life you have known and put you into the retail business, which is His. He will keep you concerned with little things in spiritual work. I think I can hear Him say to you, 'My son, keep this simplicity of spirit and just be a pastor.'"

The words speak well for the spiritual concern and clear vision of this kindly senior physician. Berggrav had really been a kind of wholesale dealer with spiritual problems, in his earliest writing, in his hectic activities in school, in his lecturing, and in his later books. He was the man who interpreted the spirit of the times, who discussed the big problems. Now he was to deal with individuals, with little problems. This was God's line. He was to try it out at Hurdal.

Hurdal was at that time a remote little place. For some reason, it belonged neither to Romerike nor Toten, and Berggrav had never had any pupils from that community in his years of teaching. It was an unknown field. Moreover, his appointment had been made in spite of the vigorously expressed wishes of the parish to have one of the other applicants instead.

Nevertheless, Berggrav was happy at Hurdal. Some of his most telling illustrations and anecdotes in later years were drawn from his experiences as a pastor here. He felt as if he had landed in exactly the right place. In a Christmas letter in 1920 he wrote, "I have it good here as a pastor. Outwardly, too good. I did not become a minister in order to find a broader field for my religious life. In a way I was entering a monastery. I am happy that I have found what I was looking for. For me it is a blessedly humble joy to do the work of the Lord in the Lord's house. I do not believe that there is any richer form of spiritual service in all our civilization."

This love for the house of the Lord was with Berggrav all through his life. Even in his period of doubt he continued to go to church, and he always got something out of it. He might feel sick or depressed before a service, but as soon as he entered the church, his illness or depression vanished. Shortly after his wife had died in 1949, he became ill on one of his official visits. Part of the program had to be canceled, but in spite of his nausea and dizziness, he wanted to take the service on the first day of Pentecost. He had to be almost carried to the car; but as soon as he had his vestments on and came before the altar, he felt better. He led the liturgy and gave the sermon with great power. Afterwards he had to be carried to the car and put to bed. This sort of thing happened many times.

To Berggrav this was an example of what the Christian life really is—God working in one's soul. If one would only reach the place which God had prepared for the work—whether in a church, at a meeting, or before the open Bible—God would take care of the rest. "Faith is an act on the part of God," he wrote once, "and so it does no good to philosophize about it; one has to get to work."

At Hurdal he quite simply *worked* for six happy years. And he and the parish understood one another. It was not all success. There were some pietists in Hurdal who would not have anything to do with the State Church and who shut him out of things. But he understood them; he saw that they were really growing in the same soil and in the same way. Therefore he felt as if they were also in "the community of saints" and he felt "happy as a daisy in the same field with these bluebells." One of the leaders of the strict *Dahlitter* sect at Hurdal wrote Berggrav many years later, "From our hearts we thank you for the fine way you dealt with us. You stuck no spokes in the wheels to hinder our work."

No, of course not. Wherever Berggrav saw genuine Christian living, it did not occur to him to act as a strict official of the State Church. He was always ecumenical at heart—especially for those with troubled hearts. In 1923 he wrote in a letter:

I sometimes feel like a complete outsider when I am with a group of believers. It hasn't been possible for me yet to appear at the pastors' annual meeting. I would feel like Saul among the prophets. . . . But when it happens, as it sometimes does in these small parishes, that I meet someone cautiously trying to confess that he is "so backward" as a Christian, then I rejoice within and I know that there is no way to measure faith or to compare life with life. I have had my best experiences with this sort of thing in these years.

The letter shows that Berggrav was not so much an ordinary country minister as he made himself out to be. The parish discovered the same thing in other ways. For one thing, Berggrav secured Sundar Singh himself—India's apostle— to visit the parish and speak in the church; so the people of Hurdal began to feel that their valley was a sort of center of culture during Berggrav's pastorate.

Then there was always "open house" at the Hurdal parsonage. All the auxiliaries met there—the Young People's League, the Ladies' Aid, the Missionary Society, the children's groups. Here the pastor and his wife brought all the old people of the parish together, after mobilizing all the cars of the valley for transportation. And here there was coffee every Sunday after church. Berggrav also worked for the building of Skrukkelia Chapel, which was dedicated in 1923. He was completely occupied with his parish work, driving around in a buggy or sleigh—later in his Ford at a killing speed

around the curving roads. There is still the saying
up there whenever a car is speeding, "That must
be either the devil or the pastor!"

Besides all this he was editing *Church and Culture*
and was preparing his doctor's dissertation, especially during the half year's leave he spent in Germany.

In spite of his being so busy, there was one thing
he put ahead of everything else—his home. In a letter from Hurdal he wrote, "My home is pure bliss."
It was at this time that he began writing "busy at
h." on his engagement calendar. If people asked him
to speak at any place on one of these days, he would
show them his calendar so they could see for themselves that it was marked "busy." He did not tell
them that "at h." meant *at home*. All ministers
might do well to take note of what Berggrav once
said about a minister's homelife:

> What else are we but whited sepulchres if we do all the
> good works of the church and are as pious as Gustav Jensen*
> but are not willing to look after our own homes? I had to
> learn this during my school years. I had to wake up. Now I
> realize it in full measure.

He often spoke to his pastors about how necessary
it is to allow some time for being at home. And
Berggrav is proof of the fact that it is possible for

---

*Gustav Jensen was dean of Christiania—and unmarried!

one to do so and still accomplish a great deal in his calling as a minister.

PRISON CHAPLAIN

In 1925 Berggrav was appointed chaplain for the Oslo Penitentiary *(Botsfengslet)*. Probably one reason for his accepting the post was the possibility of continuing his studies at the University. At any rate, he had many irons in the fire during the four years he was chaplain. He was active in the work with Christian students, had his own student circle in his home, gave lectures at the University of Oslo and at the University of Copenhagen, and fulfilled his duties as chaplain. He himself felt that he was doing too many things at one time, and in later years he reproached himself for it. In the spring of 1928 he had to take half-time leave. He himself provided for a pastor to make the cell calls for him because he was loaded down with so many other things.

Nevertheless, he came to mean a great deal to many. He prepared a special liturgy for use in the prison church. His services of worship every Sunday were unforgettable experiences, especially on such an occasion as the time he baptized his youngest son in the penitentiary, with the prisoners for the congregation. At the Wednesday meetings he always had a great deal to give, for there are few

places where one would find a more responsive
audience.

Berggrav made many friends during this period,
both among those who found themselves in prison
because of one unfortunate mistake, and among
those who went from one prison term to the next.
He also meant a great deal to those who were waiting outside—the wives and mothers of the prisoners.
He remained faithful to these friends and continued to correspond with many of them long afterward.

He wrote of these prison experiences in the book,
The Prisoner's Soul—and Our Own.

The central theme for the book is the idea he
held as a chaplain—that prisoners on the whole are
ordinary people. He stresses the fact that we outside the walls are not better than those inside—
they have given more grave expression to evil than
we have. But they also have germs of goodness and
love within them.

He points out the fact that the whole situation
of the prisoners is different from ours and that their
prison environment affects their mental and spiritual life. He tried to familiarize himself with their
circumstances so that he could understand their
reactions and help them. He understood what it
meant to be always "away," to be separated from all
homelife and natural surroundings. He realized

what it meant to be isolated and lonely, but he also saw how this loneliness could open some hearts to his ministry. He understood how difficult it is for prisoners to return to society with the prison stigma upon them. For some, their roots were pulled up forever. As he understood their problems, he applied all his psychological insight to help them.

This book was written soberly. It is a well of experiences and observations that help to explain the situation of prisoners and their reactions to these circumstances. And like his ministry at *Botsfengslet*, it is realistic yet full of human warmth.

BISHOP

It was quite a change, at the beginning of 1929, for Berggrav to pull up stakes and move to Tromsø to be a bishop. But he was soon at work and going at top speed.

There was no lack of initial difficulties. Although he had the largest number of pastoral votes, he had been only third in the total votes, and there were many who met him with distrust. He was a liberal, they thought, and sometimes he got to hear that he was not a real Christian. In the midst of this distrust, his old doubts would reappear; and he experienced what he was to call later "the winter-dark days of his soul."

A bishop is in an exposed position, and Berggrav
was a sensitive man. He took all criticism personally, and his self-reproach was beyond all reason. Still
he did not become more cautious. He had no faculty
for protecting himself, either against hasty speech
and action or against criticism afterwards. Yet the
fact that he was not always on guard made
friends for him. If anyone ever discovered how
hypersensitively defenseless this great man was, he
became a friend for life. Only, not everybody took
time to discover this secret—or Berggrav did not
give them the opportunity to find out.

He was under great strain, for example, in 1933
during the Norwegian controversy about the play,
The Green Pastures. The National Theater wanted
to put on the play, but there was a storm of protest
from Christians who believed that it was blasphe-
mous to have our Lord appear upon the stage as He
would have to in this Negro play. Berggrav had seen
the play in Stockholm; and in a personal letter to a
good friend who was a Theater Board member, he
had said that he saw nothing offensive in the play
if a few scenes were omitted. The letter was read at
a meeting of the steering committee of the National
Theater, and then the hullabaloo started. Berggrav
spoke out in self-defense in the *Evening Paper,* but
he found little understanding among church people
for his opinion or for his having interfered in the

matter at all. He had not done so intentionally, of
course, but had merely expressed his opinion in a
personal letter without, however, taking the pre-
caution to keep it from publication. We should add
that after the war, when *The Green Pastures* was
presented at the National Theater, not a voice was
raised in protest. But back in 1933 it had been inti-
mated that Berggrav should resign as bishop because
he had defended the play.

This was the second time that Berggrav had
found himself on the firing line in a national controversy, the first time having been in connection
with the Østland Revolt. Nor was this the last time.
Norwegian newspaper debates are not even-tem-
pered affairs, and they certainly were never such
for Berggrav. He suffered many cuts and some
deep wounds, but strangely they left no scars. He
never carried a grudge, and he could show by a
quick, warm handshake that he was still a good
friend, even to those who attacked him most.

All these controversies affected his work as a
bishop. It took time for him to win the confidence
of the devout Christians. But he won it in the end,
and what swept away all opposition was his *preaching*.

You may say what you will about narrow-mind-
ed Norwegians, but what determines their judgment of a churchman is his preaching. If they catch

the right tone in the sermon, then his preaching is
right, and their hearts melt—no matter what they
may think of his views on culture or shall we say
on his judgment of a Negro play with our Lord
the leading character!

Almost all Norwegians now living have had an
opportunity to hear Berggrav preach. When he
spoke over the radio, there was a drop in church
attendance as people stayed at home to hear Berggrav. And yet there are not many who have heard
him at his best. He could be great on great occasions; but he was at his best on lesser occasions that
did not call for a bishop as speaker but simply a
pastor preaching the Word of God.

He has said that it was the Danish Olfert
Ricard who taught him to preach. And it was
probably from Ricard that he got his first inspiration. But Berggrav became more and more free
from artifice as he continued to preach. He also
showed less and less the psychological bent he had
in the beginning, although he was often subjective
and deeply personal in his preaching. He was really
more like J. J. Jansen, whose one rule was, "Every
word must live before it is spoken."

That is why Berggrav could fascinate people. If
there is anything that will make people pay attention to a sermon, it is the feeling that the preacher
himself has experienced what he is talking about.

Berggrav was always realistic, true to life in his preaching. He talked about tangible things and used concrete examples so that everyone could understand him.

This was Berggrav's strength as a preacher. If he had any weakness, it was in the opposite direction.

The purpose of preaching is to bring the Word of God to the hearts of men. Here then, are the two obligations of the preacher: (1) to reach down into the hearts of people, and this Berggrav could do as few others ever could; and (2) to preach the Word of God as it is written, and this was his difficulty. One could see that sometimes Berggrav hesitated to deal with texts that he thought some people would find hard to understand. The hesitancy was partly the result of the times in which he lived and of the religious crisis through which he had passed; but it is also a part of the lot of all of us preachers. It *is* hard to preach on all texts with equal eagerness and joy. What are we to say on such questions as the second coming of Christ? And what about the destruction the Bible predicts?

Berggrav grappled with these questions, especially the latter. What helped him to an answer here was his "helpless loyalty to the words of Jesus." He could not help bringing to others the things that Jesus had said.

After the middle '30's his preaching took on a

more evangelical tone. Under the impact of the
Oxford Movement he had experienced what it
means to be a sinner justified. No one I have
heard could speak more movingly about justifica-
tion. It was not only that one's sins have been for-
given. Berggrav knew that it also meant that one
has been set free from self and can thus lead a new
life, not on the basis of what one is, but on the basis
of what God in Christ has said that he is. "When
God looks at me," he said in a sermon, "He does
not see me—and thank God for that—but He sees
Christ in my heart. And then I am just as precious
to Him as His own beloved Son."

The keynote of his preaching was simply this—
the pure gospel. With its message he reached out to
all people. And with its grace he finally reached
into the hearts of the believers.

One can hardly overestimate the significance of
Berggrav as a preacher. For a number of years he
was the center of the church's defense against
secularism. At a time when most of the people had
begun to look upon the church and Christianity as
heirlooms now obsolete, Berggrav managed to open
the ears of people to the fact that the church still
had something vitally important to say to them.
Conditions had been threatening to set believing
Christians apart like a small island in a secularized
ocean of people; but Berggrav could show them

that Christianity is something that concerns all people. Here was the reason that the church became such a strong force during the war. Berggrav's preaching helped strengthen its position, for he made the church timely for everyone. Even those who were critical of his popular preaching benefited from it. They could spread their sails under the shelter of the far-flung effectiveness Berggrav gave the church. He had this power to strengthen and build up, all his life, in all that he did, but it was particularly evident in his preaching.

His radio ministry was especially effective—both his lectures and his services of worship. He reached the largest circle of listeners with his program, "Answers to Questions About Religion."* During the heated debates about hell, he went right ahead, discussing the most controversial questions and doing much to clarify the problems. Without letting himself become confused by the many "stars" in the controversy, he made very clear the serious words of Jesus on perdition.

Probably not many of his sermons will go down in history. They were geared to their own times, and only a few of them were ever printed. But he preached the Word of God as it was meant to be preached, and that is the real task of the preacher.

---

*Published in book form in 1953, under the title *Religionen og vi.*

As a church officer and administrator Berggrav
was very good. He had a natural gift for that kind
of work. After he became bishop, old bureaucratic
customs disappeared fast from the Hålogaland
office. The official correspondence of all the pastors
goes through the Bishop's office; and his opinion is
required on everything—applications, appoint-
ments, inquiries from church councils, church
building projects, questions about parsonages, and
the like. Berggrav had a practical way of dealing
with all such matters. He could see the point of a
problem at once. He knew all the complicated
church laws by heart. He was at that time both
administrator and preacher, and his official visitations around the parishes gave him a store of interesting experiences.

In his eight years in Hålogaland he made over a
hundred visitations. Each visit lasted anywhere
from 2 or 3 days to 8 or 9. He visited each parish
once and managed a second visit for about a fourth
of them. It was an extremely large district which,
since that time, has been divided into two dioceses.
Many Norwegians do not realize that the mid-point
between Lindesnes and the North Cape is Mo in
Rana, which is 100 miles north of the southern
border of Hålogaland.

When Berggrav became Bishop of Oslo in September, 1937, there were 137 places to visit in

the Oslo Diocese, which had not yet been divided. With the stipulation that each parish must be visited at least once every six years, this meant that Berggrav must visit 23 parishes each year. It proved to be an impossible task. In 1938 and 1939 he made 19 visits each year. But during the War years, with so many extra demands especially upon the Bishop of Oslo, besides his three years of imprisonment, Berggrav had fallen far behind in his rounds of visitation. In 1948 Tunsberg Diocese was separated from Oslo. But even in that year there were ten places in the Diocese and several parishes in the city of Oslo that he did not get to visit.

He was very unhappy that he had not been able to complete the rounds, and he would not listen to all the excuses people made for him. It was part of his official duty, he thought, and it really ought to be done, even though he did not think that the bishops' visits played too important a role in the church.

This point has been much debated, and the bishop himself is probably not a good person to judge the effectiveness of his visits. Those who know the conditions in Denmark will realize how disastrous it has been that visitations have been discontinued there. The bishop is the unifying influence in the church. If his visitations stop, there is danger that each parish may do as it pleases, and that the church will become just a collection of parishes. The inspection of the parishes is important in itself. Besides that, there is the supervision of the liturgy and preaching, as well as the development of parish affairs. When the bishop comes to visit, all the weaknesses in parish life can be taken up and talked over. Berggrav was often able to clear up difficulties of a personal nature on his parish visits.

Of most importance is the fact that the visitation is a source of inspiration to the faithful core of the congregation. During the visit all the members, especially those who seldom attend services, will come to church; and the result is that the congregation comes into closer contact with all the people of the community.

An important feature of the visitation is the bishop's meeting with the church council. What is discussed there becomes the basis for the bishop's impression of the condition of the parish and also furnishes him with the material for his talk at the parish visitation meeting.

Berggrav soon found that it did not do very well to send his questions to the church council in advance. If he did, the answers were likely to be cautious and formal. So he usually waited and put his questions to the council orally, thus giving each member a chance to "speak his piece."

The following questions taken from his notes indicate the kind of questions he used to ask:

I. *On drinking*
    1. Decline or progress since last visitation?
    2. Reasons for this?
    3. Particular circumstances: Home-brewing? Illegal liquor selling? Drunkenness at parties? Holidays? Funerals? (Sic!) Athletic meets, especially night games?
    4. Opinion about drunkenness?

II. *On the young people, 16-20-year group*
    1. In general: Any complaints about embarrassing behavior?
    2. Interests? What do they read? How do they like to work? Unemployment?
    3. Liberal leagues? Dancing uppermost? Rules for parties? Other humanitarian youth work?
    4. Christian youth work?

III. *Home and children, 4-15 years*
    1. Are the children taking over the control?
    2. Does the family have their meals together?
    3. Adolescent children, newly confirmed?

IV. *Home and devotional life*
    1. Grace and evening prayer?
    2. Radio listening and devotions—is radio just on, or is it used for home devotions?
    3. Reading and singing? weekdays? Sunday?
    4. Sunday school: In the church? By organizations? The Salvation Army?

V. *Lay preaching*
    1. Many traveling evangelists?
    2. Attendance at meetings? Decreased? Increased? Stable? Critical view?

    3. Effects? Tired of meetings?

    4. Are there local speakers? Giving witness? Local talents?

VI. *Sanctuaries and cemeteries*

    1. Condition and upkeep of churches?

    2. Is the warden doing his duty? Who is the warden?

    3. How many does the church seat?

    4. Is it kept clean?

    5. Does the council see to it that the cemetery and the registry of graves are in order?

VII. *Church attendance*

    1. Has church attendance declined? Increased? Remained the same? Any difference according to seasons? Best attendance when? Baptism during service?

    2. Approximate attendance on normal Sundays?

    3. Arrangement for a church bus?

    4. Are there many persons who never come to church during the year?

    5. Does the service begin on time? Is the Altar Book followed? Is there an organist?

    6. Do people stay in the church until the close of the service? What are their manners in church? How is the behavior on Confirmation Day?

    7. At the minister's meetings outside the church how is the attendance? Sunday mornings? Other times?

    8. How are the services apportioned within the parish?

VIII. *Moral conditions within the congregations?*

    1. Unbaptized children?

    2. Unconfirmed persons?

    3. Immorality? *(Konkubinater)*

    4. Keeping Sunday peace? Sunday funerals?

    5. Civil funerals and marriages?

IX. *Christian organizations*

    1. Do humanitarian organizations take the upper hand?

2. What about growth? Any young people coming in?
3. Is it mostly older folks who are interested?
4. Relationship of the organizations *to* the church? Among themselves?

X. *Dissenters*
1. How many and what kind?
2. Any wind in their sails?
3. Their relationship with the church?
4. Do their children take religious instruction in the schools?
5. The Salvation Army?

XI. *Reverence for holiness*
1. Any change noted? Direct resistance? Scorn? Against the church? The clergy? Against the Christian faith?
2. What about swearing?

XII. *Neighborhood relations and crime*
1. When anyone is in trouble?
2. Gossip and litigation? Hotheaded people?
3. Lawbreaking and crime?
4. Child welfare cases?

XIII. *Parish and parish council*
1. How often do they meet?
2. Has the council started any Christian work? See the rules for parish councils, No. 7.
3. Has the council tried to fulfill No. 11? (It is the duty of the council to give attention to everything that can be done to promote Christian life within the parish, especially to see that the Word of God is well preached, that it is brought to the sick and the dying, that young people are brought into good causes and that their physical and spiritual needs are provided for. The council may assign members or appoint committees to fulfill such duties volun-

tarily and to help conduct such activities within
the council.)

4. Is there a parish treasury?

5. Is there anything that is being neglected in the
parish? Anything fallen into disuse? What is the
greatest weakness of this parish? What are you most
happy about? What are the next projects to be
undertaken?

6. The relationship between the pastor and the parish: I assume that there is a good relationship here.
But with all of us, there are some things that we
need to be made aware of. If there is anything of the
sort here, then you should tell it to your pastor
some time when I am not here. If it is said in
my presence, it may seem like a complaint, and
that is not likely to help matters. If there is
something that you ought to talk over with your
pastor in a friendly way, then *do* it. If you don't,
then you will fail both in your duty to love one
another and in your duties as servants of the congregation.

XIV. *Attendance at communion*

1. How many communicants are there? How many
communion services during the year? Outside of
the church? Do you use individual cups?

2. Are there many Christians who do not take communion? Their reasons?

3. Do the young people come to communion? Men?
Women?

4. Do you use confession?

This form of questioning was not followed word
for word, but it was the basis for discussing the
parish and its situation. Many of the questions were
taken from the old regulations regarding parish
visitation. Others, like XIV, 2, grew out of Berg-

grav's own experiences. He might find some persons like that in the parish council, and such a question might lead to a personal conversation between them and their bishop.

One can see that the visitor would get an exhaustive picture of the parish, and it does not take much imagination to see what use Berggrav could make of his information when he presented his visitation message to the church. Someone said once of such a meeting, "He talked as if he knew everything about this place." And that was the way it was.

We note that these questions charged the congregation with the responsibility for the spiritual needs of the whole local populace. So the visitation of the bishop came to be a flagday for the community church idea.

A compact little report of each visit can be found in Berggrav's visitation books, dry and concise, but filled with glimpses of typical parish life.

If anything was wrong, he reproved it sharply, saying, for example, "No other church in the diocese is so poorly kept up as this one. The question is, do you want to have a church, or don't you care at all?" Such words speeded up improvement, though not always without a squabble.

But if Berggrav met a situation where there was nothing to be done about it, he acted quite differently. On one occasion a new chapel was to be dedicated. The local people had wanted to have it inside the churchyard cemetery, but the bishop *advised* and the Department *decided* that it should be built outside. Nevertheless it was built inside the churchyard, and Berggrav did not know anything about it until he went over the evening before the dedication to see that everything was in order. He was astonished, but he said not a word about it. As he walked about the church he moved the altar candlesticks a little to make them more symmetrically placed. The chairman of the building committee said, "So? The Bishop is moving the candlesticks?" To which Berggrav replied quickly with a smile, "Can't I move a few candlesticks if you can move a whole church?" And so the matter was settled, to the great relief of those who were going about with a pretty uneasy conscience.

The visitations were often festive occasions for Berggrav, like his famous trip to Karasjok in March, 1930. Both the Bishop and his wife were riding in a sleigh pulled by a reindeer over the Finnmark plains, and time after time Berggrav had to jump from his sleigh because of a black dog that kept frightening his reindeer although it paid no attention to the reindeer of the parish pastor who was traveling with them. Great was Berggrav's delight when he finally got the dog to jump at the

other reindeer so that the president had to roll out
into the snow too. The dog became a legend with
Berggrav, especially after it appeared in church at
the visitation service there at Karasjok. It met the
Bishop at the church steps and finally lay down
under the pulpit as quiet as a mouse when Berggrav
began to preach. The Bishop never tired of telling
about its tricks. In fact, all Karasjok had grown so
accustomed to the stories of the black dog that
when on the last day of the visit they were all at
dinner with one of the families, the host's tongue
slipped at the conclusion of his tribute to the Bishop,
saying, *"Skål da, bisken"** instead of *"Skål da,
Bisp!"*****

The visitations were a tremendous strain when
there was something seriously wrong with the pastor and the parish. In one of his letters he describes
a visit to such a church. In the conclusion he wrote
as follows:

> Just think of traveling to that congregation! Processes are
> being served; there are charges and countercharges, no end
> of complaints to the bishop. Between you and me, I come to
> such a visit with an entirely different kind of calmness than
> I have at other times. The task is so immense, so far beyond
> my ability to handle that the only thing I can do is pray.
> How did it go? Well, I must say that *it came*. It takes all
> one's imagination and downright wisdom to know where to

Bisk is a pet name for dog, corresponding to "doggie."
***Bisp*, Bishop.

make the right turn. But this is the main point. My first objective is to find *something good,* partly because I know there is always some good everywhere, and partly because I have to feel kindly toward a group before I can speak any words of admonition to them. . . . Then one evening one of the most irate men of the group came to talk with me. It became a meeting of reconciliation. I drew up a document and got them to sign and to solemnly promise to withdraw the charge for criminal action and the charge of libel.

I cannot say what is accomplished on such a visitation. But my endeavor is the greatest I can make it. And in a way it is one of my greatest hours when I feel my ego dethroned and myself utterly dependent—even with my abilities strained to the uttermost.

This particular visitation ended with Berggrav speaking on the Lord's Supper. "Then I felt how all the paths turned inward; there was a feeling of unity over it all, and all dissentions seemed to have disappeared."

Of course there were ups and down on these visitations. Things did not always go so well. But when he did succeed, he could begin a "new era" for the parish, getting it off to a brand new start; and the effects were noticeable for years to come.

An essential element in a bishop's life is his relationship with the ministers under him. In his 21 years as bishop Berggrav ordained 156 pastors, 34 of them in Hålogaland. Besides these there were all the bishops' ordinations that he performed as Bishop of Oslo.

It is required by law for all ministers to have an

interview with their bishop before they are ordained. This was once called the Bishop's Examination. Before the interview each candidate had
to fill out a questionnaire, in which he was to
give a detailed account of his life and a history of
his entire theological development. Two things
were of especial importance to Berggrav: first, he
wanted to get to know the candidate for ordination
personally; and second, he wanted to find out if
there was anything in the teachings of the church
that was still not clear to the candidate. One of the
standard questions concerned the young minister's
views on *objective redemption*. He wanted to be
sure that the central point was clearly understood
and adhered to.

The personal nature of the interview also had an
effect on the ordination service. Berggrav introduced a new custom here. Previously, the oldest
candidate gave the ordination sermon. But now all
the candidates came to the chancel door with the
Bishop. Berggrav would ask each one in turn
whether there was some passage from the Bible that
had especial meaning for him. Each replied briefly,
and in this way each one had a chance to say something; and at the same time the congregation had
a glimpse into the personalities of all the candidates.

Of especial importance to the pastors under him
was the Retreat which Berggrav arranged for them

every year, beginning in 1946. For two or three
days they would all meet at the Klækken Hotel in
Ringerike. There they had an opportunity to visit
and to talk about their problems. Berggrav ran it in
"boarding-school" style, and saw to it that everyone felt at home. The social hours were just for
pleasant fellowship, and laughter echoed through
the rooms. At the same time it was a purposeful
meeting and there was an air of genuine sincerity
about it. Berggrav wanted the men to learn something, too; and so he engaged special speakers for
the Retreat. One year, for instance, he secured three
physicians as speakers.

There were those who thought that Berggrav had
too little time to give to his pastors, and there may
have been some truth in that. He had so many irons
in the fire, especially after he came to Oslo! But
then, too, he was not the kind of person that everyone took a liking to at first sight, mainly—I think—
because of his natural shyness or reticence.

But it is also true that his concern was almost
boundless when anything was really wrong, and
that is when a minister needs his bishop the most.
As a counselor, sitting face to face with one in
trouble, all the formality of "bishop" disappeared
and he talked as one poor sinner with another. If it
was necessary to get at the heart of a difficulty, he
could be sharp as a surgeon's knife; then once the

sore spot was laid bare, he was gentle as healing balm, pouring the warmth of the gospel over anyone who realized his sin or neglect.

Berggrav was never one to sit and wait to be sought out by those in trouble. As soon as he sensed that someone was in difficulty or in sorrow, he would break away from whatever he was busy with and travel any distance to see if he could be of help. Even in his student years, he made sudden trips to help or comfort friends in trouble far away. He knew how it helps to have friends close by when one is hurt or grieved. This sort of assistance he was continually giving, not only to pastors but to many, many others. In time of sorrow he was a comforter; in affliction he was a supporter. But when anyone had done wrong, he could be a surgeon. He did not hesitate to tell the truth face to face. Perhaps it smarted, and some could not take it. Others realized the truth of his words, "You can still be happy so long as there is anyone who cares enough to scold you!"

LEADER IN THE CHURCH

A leader is not a person who can do everything best of all himself. A leader is one who can inspire those working with him to do *their* best and who can keep them working together.

Berggrav became such a leader. In 1929 he was the youngest member of the College of Bishops. He was only forty-four, and there is reason to believe that his older colleagues looked upon him with some skepticism. His election had been close; besides, they knew his journalistic style and his often boyish manner.

Nevertheless, as the youngest member, he was appointed at once to take the minutes at the bishops' meetings. As a result, the wording of the resolutions was often left to him. He immediately proved to be a keen co-worker. He managed to find the right wording for each opinion and was a master at choosing a wording that all of them would approve.

One principle dominated Berggrav's conscious program as a leader of the church: The church must be united and strong. All unnecessary disagreements were to be disposed of; all hidden suspicions were to be cleared up. One may say that Berggrav was a compromiser if we understand that a compromise, instead of being a threat to society, may be the only fair and proper solution to a difficult situation.

It was an exhilarating experience to meet with Berggrav in a committee or at a board meeting, especially in one or another under-cover commit-

tee during the War. First of all, he always created a
pleasant, confident atmosphere. He talked openly
about everything, but he never acted cocksure. He
wanted everybody to get a word in. He always began by listening. Then he could quickly sense what
each person had in mind, and in a way identify
himself with it. Then his own statement would
come, and usually most of the others would find
their views incorporated in it.

All this is, of course, in accordance with good
democratic procedures, except that Berggrav's was
a lively kind of democracy. He could not stand a
dry discussion. A "debate-and-vote" church meeting was a horror to him. He understood that the
minority wants to be right about something, too,
and he wanted something of their opinion to be included in any resolution.

So he became the great Joint Council leader.

The Christian Joint Council was formed at his
suggestion. On his way home from church at
Stavanger, September 3, 1939, he and Dean Kornelius learned from a man on the street that England
had declared war. As they walked on, talking together, they agreed that all the Christians in Norway must stand together and that an open appeal
must be made about it to all the Norwegian people. Kornelius was, at that time, chairman of the

Joint Council of Organizations,* and Berggrav
asked him if he would be willing to sign such an
appeal in the name of the JCO, together with
Berggrav.

Kornelius had to decline. He was willing enough
as a private person, but as chairman of the Council
he had no authority to act on behalf of the others.
And the vice-chairman was Ole Hallesby!

Hallesby had expressed his disapproval very
sharply when Berggrav had been appointed Bishop
of Oslo two years before, and Berggrav and others
that he spoke to thought it highly unlikely that
Hallesby would be a co-signer of the appeal together with Berggrav. Berggrav had been a Liberal
and had never retracted anything!

When Berggrav returned to Oslo, he cut short
dubious deliberations, picked up the telephone, and
called Hallesby, whom he had met only once in the
past twelve years. (Such was the situation in the
church at that time.) Hallesby's reply was very
friendly. He asked if he might hear the proposed
appeal which had been worked out in deliberations
with other members of the Council.

"It all appeals to me very much," said Hallesby.

---

*The Joint Council of Organizations is a co-operative committee com-
posed of most of the nationwide Christian organizations within the Norwegian Church, with the Inner Mission, the Mission Society, and the
Seamen's Mission as the leading groups.

"I should like to think it over. You will hear from me within half an hour."

Fearful of having been misunderstood, Berggrav hastened to make sure that Hallesby realized that the appeal would bear only two signatures, Hallesby's and Berggrav's. Yes, that was clear to him.

After half an hour Hallesby called. He wanted to hear the text of the document once more. Berggrav offered to take a taxi and bring a copy to him. "No," replied Hallesby, "that would be too far for you. Just read it to me once more." After the reading came the reply, short and hearty, "Surely, I will sign it."

The next day, September 6, the appeal appeared in newspapers all over the Nordic countries. The wording itself was not epoch-making. It was an appeal to all Christians to unite in prayer and repentance and to be deeply aware of the responsibility that the gravity of war laid upon the church. But the two signatures standing side by side—that was the beginning of a new era. They were the symbols of the two divisions of the Norwegian Church: The Church of the People *(Folkekirken)* and the Laymen's Revival *(Legmannsvekkelsen)*. Once more the Church was united and strong, and people looked with new hope to the Christian Church.

The Appeal also brought about the formation of the Christian Joint Council which was organized a year later, after Terboven's speech on September 25, 1940, had marked the beginning of the Nazifying process. (Terboven was the Reich Commissioner in Norway during the occupation.) Again it was Berggrav who had taken the initiative. On October 16 he called on Hallesby and outlined the situation: Now both the church and civil life were about to be Nazified; now they would all have to stand together. Hallesby immediately agreed, and it was not long before the two of them were at the very center of the movement.

"But the China Mission will never go along with us," Hallesby believed.* The China Mission—the Norwegian Lutheran Missionary Society—was noted for its opposition to all Liberals and for its low-church leanings and its distrust of anything that smacked of a bishop-controlled church. It was not a member of the Joint Council of Organizations.

"Just wait till tomorrow," Berggrav replied.

Next day when he rang the doorbell at the home of the head of the China Society, Ludwig Hope, the latter met him at the door with the words, "I have been waiting for you."

---

*See the account in "When the Fight Came," p. 106, *Country and Church (Land og Kirke, 1945).*

It took only a half hour for the two men to reach an understanding, and from then on these three—Berggrav, Hallesby, and Hope—were the leaders of the fight waged by the Norwegian Church against Naziism. They differed widely, but at the same time this triumvirate comprised the three keenest, strongest leaders of Norwegian Christendom.

The other permanent members of the Joint Council were Ragnvald Indrebø, Kristian Hansson, Ingvald B. Carlsen, Hans Høeg, and H. E. Wisløff. Superintendent Smeby was a member, but he passed away early in the struggle. General Secretary Amdahl of the Missionary Society took part in the meetings whenever he was in Oslo; and on important occasions, Mr. Lavik, Member of Parliament, was present.

The plan [of organization] was approved at a meeting in the Bishop's residence in Oslo on October 25. It had been confirmed at a meeting of the bishops a few days earlier. It was presented to the public at a big meeting held at the Calmeyer Street Mission House on October 28, 1940. Here Hallesby, Hope, and Bishops Støren and Berggrav spoke; and the huge audience understood that the Church was really in earnest about its resistance to Naziism and that all Christians must stand together in this struggle.

The meeting was a significant one for a whole
generation of Christians in Norway. For in spite
of the fact that after the War some controversies
and misunderstandings reappeared, those of us who
were present at that first meeting will never forget
the spirit of brotherhood that prevailed. Many of
us think of it now in the words of Bjørnson:

> There rose over the mountain a vision aglow
> To urge us to struggle to death with the foe.

Of course it was not possible with one stroke to
win complete confidence in the new unity in the
Church—something so contrary to the differences
that had appeared at that former meeting in the
Mission House back in 1920. There was some alarm,
especially in Westland—had the Liberals now been
accepted? Ludwig Hope was furious, and he and
Berggrav went about holding meetings with various
groups. Then the Joint Christian Council, in a supplementary declaration, explained that the estab-
lishment of the Joint Council did not mean an
armistice with those who attacked the old faith.
People were still free to argue with each other on
questions about their faith.

The union was also hard for some old Liberals
to swallow. Was Berggrav surrendering to Hallesby
and Hope? Was he renouncing his Liberal past?

Berggrav insisted that he had nothing to re-

nounce, and rightly so. The problems posed by the
Liberal theologians had never been his problems. In
1927 he had been a driving force in opposition to
that group's religio-political organization, the Norwegian pastors' progressive group.

The solution to the threatening conflict was typical of Berggrav. He had never been a supporter of
any one particular group in the Norwegian Church.
He identified himself with the Church as it was,
and he wanted to be its servant. He would rather
take blows from each side—as is always the lot of
the conciliator. Berggrav wanted one thing above
all others—complete reconciliation between the
conflicting factions of the Church. This was typical
of his attitude toward the Church in the 1950's.

Within the Christian Council, too, Berggrav
held the position of coordinator. The seriousness of
the situation brought the members together in a
close Christian friendship that outlasted the war.
After the Joint Council no longer needed to function, the members met together just the same, and
just the knowing that these leaders were meeting to
talk things over had a beneficial effect upon the
Church. It was good to know that the important
churchmen were on speaking terms.

It has not always been that way in the Norwegian Church; and the time may come when it will
be so no longer. But at least we can remember that

Church unity was close to Berggrav's heart. He realized that the Church is not an institution, but a fellowship of Christian people, and that it is downright sinful if these people cannot talk things over frankly. There may be some differences that no joint council and no joint prayer can overcome—deep fundamental differences. Berggrav was not blind to them. But he always wanted people to try talking them out. He believed in a sacrament of friendship, and for the sake of this belief he often underwent great personal humiliation.

He was no self-appointed chieftain, nor did he want to be. He was a joint-councilman and therefore a great leader in the Church.

His term as Bishop became a period of peace and cooperation in the Norwegian Church. It was not by accident that no open controversies broke out within the Church during those years. Many were the times that he tempered passions without ever sacrificing the truth. So these years marked a period of progress in the Church.

By virtue of his office, Berggrav had his fingers in almost everything that happened, and it would be impossible to enumerate all his enterprises. We should mention, however, that during his imprisonment he worked out a proposal for the reorganization of the Church of Norway, and that after the war he became chairman of the committee that

worked on a joint program designed to give the
Church more independence from the State. Not
much was left of the original proposal when Parliament finally adopted it. But it marked the end of
one line of endeavor in Berggrav's life as a leader
of the Church.

As early as the '30's Berggrav had engaged in a
debate with the head of the Church Department
through the pages of *Church and Culture,* during
which he defended the rights of the Church over
against the rights of the State. He drew his arguments from the fields of theology, history, and
church law. When he began to write *The Foundation of the Church* in 1942, he had the whole background ready.

It was not because Berggrav wanted a church
dominated by bishops that he emphasized the importance of the bishops' meetings; it was because
the bishops' meetings provided the only organ to
speak for the Church. He showed that he wanted
to include the laity in his plan for the Joint Christian Council and also in his plan of organization
for the Church. His last effort in this direction
was the book *Contra Castberg,* 1953, which spoke
out sharply against the purely State's-rights way
of thinking.

Berggrav was of course a man of the State
Church. He did not want separation from the State.

But in all his work as Bishop we note his desire for independence for the Church and his efforts to provide organs for Church action. But if the Church was ever to *act* effectively she must find herself in agreement in all her branches. And so, to Berggrav, joint deliberation and power to act were two sides of the same cause.

And the cause was: The Church of Norway at work for the soul of Norway.

Chapter Nine

The War

"HAVE you noticed how full of life the Bible has become?" Berggrav said on April 14, 1940. "It is as if it is written for people in war and during times of occupation." Then he read from the prophet Habakkuk 1:5-11. Anyone who looks up the verses will see how well they fitted the Germans in those days: " . . . who march through the breadth of the earth, to seize habitations not their own. . . . They scoff at kings . . . whose own might is their god!"

Berggrav himself was full of life during the War. He was made for just such a situation. In fact he suited the times of war almost better than the times of peace.

ATTEMPTS FOR PEACE
1939-1940

We know now that our whole attempt for peace was futile. Yes, we even know that Hitler's war had to be fought to the bitter end. No one could make a treaty of peace with Hitler. But this present knowledge should not prevent us from understanding those who tried in 1939 to make "peace at once," as Berggrav had worded it. The movement began, as did the Christian Joint Council, with the "Appeal" of Berggrav and Hallesby, issued September 6, 1939. Johan H. Andresen, a manufacturer, had read this strong manifestation of Christian unity, and together with the famous painter, Henrik Sørensen, he called on Berggrav that very evening.

The three reached an understanding among themselves, and began what they called a "Defense League for Peace." It became very important, and it took up a great deal of Berggrav's time up to the moment that Norway was drawn into the war in 1940. In speaking about the close cooperation of these three leaders, Berggrav wrote in the fall of 1939, "Sørensen is the mainspring in the clockwork, Andresen is the pendulum, and I am the hand."

Berggrav had the background for such work. He had long been active in the World Alliance which aimed to promote friendship among the nations through their churches. It had been organized in 1914, the day after the outbreak of World War I; and its purpose at first was to maintain contacts across the fronts through connections with the churches. Even at that time Berggrav was enthusiastic about the work and was strongly critical of those who scoffed at work for peace.

In January, 1939, this World Alliance had held a meeting in London. Because of crucial international developments, a special executive committee was formed with Berggrav as chairman. Thus he had some authority from religious denominations all over the world, and he felt an obligation to those who had elected him to make an effort for peace.

He has written a report of what was accomplished. It is as exciting reading as a novel and should be published sometime. The climaxes are three interviews: the first with the British Minister of Foreign Affairs, Lord Halifax, December 15, 1939; the second with Herman Göring on January 21, 1940; and the third with Lord Halifax again on January 27, 1940.

The main difficulty in arranging a peace was not in drawing up the terms themselves, for there were private communications from Berlin's Department of Foreign Affairs giving the terms that Germany would consider as practicable for peace. The main points were that the Czechs were to regain their independence, Slovakia was to become independent, and Poland was to be a free nation once more but with the western boundary she had had in 1914. These conditions had been drafted in a *pro memoria,* and it was with this document in his pocket that Berggrav made his three trips.

Far more important than the terms themselves were guarantees that they would be kept. Could anyone trust Hitler? Berggrav himself did not think so, but he made the bold venture of trying his fortunes with Göring, whom he chose to meet instead of Hitler.

It is easy to be wise after the fact, especially after the right side has won the war. The picture would be totally different if we had had enough imagination to perceive that the situation at that time was not unlike our situation today. That is, there was a kind of cold war going on during the winter of 1939-1940. One realized the horrors that total war would bring. Was not peace to be preferred, even if it meant only a postponement of war? Would anyone refuse today to try to arrange a summit meeting?

Here is what Berggrav was planning. Secret negotiations were to be arranged before the war had become so terrible that one side had the upper hand and would force the fight to the bitter end.

Berggrav's descriptions of Göring and his tre-

mendous Karin Hall are interesting reading. It
seems evident that Göring was a somewhat more
reasonable man than the other Nazi leaders. However, he was bound by his "Germanic oath to the
Führer," as he expressed it to Berggrav in strong
Nazi tones. Then he added in a whisper, "But we
consult with each other on all matters. The Führer
says, 'My dear Göring, what do you say to this?'
I will do my best. But I am not the one who will
make the decision."

Berggrav's impression of Göring was that he was
two persons, one rather reasonable and the other
tied body and soul to Hitler.

But the whole plan was wrecked by Lord Halifax
because he wanted to have guarantees in the form
of action. Germany would have to evacuate Poland
and Czechoslovakia before the negotiations could
begin.

Berggrav must have been a master negotiator. He
had hour-long interviews with both men. He "took
a lot" from each man, but he also returned some
good, firm words.

It was an achievement in itself to gain admittance
to both officials. He managed it through his church
contacts. His account of his first encounter with
Bishop Bell* in London is a stirring narrative. Berg-

*This account appears in Berggrav's obituary of Bell in the *Ecumenical
Review,* January 1959

grav was introduced to Bell on his mission to London in December, 1939. Bell said at once: "Let us first pray together and later talk about the matter." The two bishops knelt together on the floor, and from that moment they were friends and co-workers for the rest of their lives. In midst of the War they kept in touch. And even if their first attempts for peace were in vain, they did not give up. All through the War years they saw to it that contacts were maintained with churchmen from all the nations in the conflict. Berggrav was absorbed in this work even during his imprisonment, with heart and soul keeping track of the secret meetings held in Sweden.

Berggrav realized that many might call his attempts for peace in 1939 and 1940 ludicrous. But he liked to quote a fellow-worker from his years as prison chaplain. When people hesitated about putting a prisoner on probation for fear the man might fail, this worker would say, "If no one is willing to take a ducking, no one will ever be rescued."

During that critical winter Berggrav went several times to Holland, England, Germany, Switzerland, Stockholm, and Copenhagen. His journeys were concerned not only with negotiations for peace, but also with aid to refugees, aid to Finland, meetings with churchmen from many countries. The Chris-

tian Brothers' Aid had been organized at the Bishop's residence November 9, 1939. A Nordic church
conference was held at Oslo in November. Here the
Nordic churches invited discussions with English,
French, and German churchmen. At the first joint
meeting Nordic church leaders conferred with
leaders from French and English churches in Holland in January. The Germans were content to
invite Berggrav to a conference at Berlin.

Berggrav began to gain an international name.
When he was imprisoned later, becoming a personal
symbol of the resistance of the Norwegian Church,
he found it helpful to have met so many of Europe's
churchmen.

Even he at length became disheartened by the
hopelessness of his cause and worn out by so much
traveling. While he was still in the midst of it, he
was interviewed by a reporter in Copenhagen and
asked whether he intended to take up Archbishop
Söderblom's efforts for peace. With great conviction, Berggrav replied, "No, I haven't the dimensions for it!"

But he was wrong about that. Dimensions are
not measured by results, but according to one's
courage and the will to go ahead. These traits he
had already demonstrated. His greatest test was
close at hand.

NORWAY IN THE FIRST YEAR
OF THE WAR

In his book, *When the Fight Came*, Berggrav has
described with minute accuracy his experiences
from April 9, 1940, up to his *Pastoral Letter* and its
fate in February 1941. Instead of repeating his account here, it may be illuminating to see what one
of his fellow-workers, Ferdinand Schjeldrup, Judge
of the Supreme Court, has written in his book, *On
the Broad Front*, 1947 (page 55):

Berggrav's ability to react spontaneously, which sometimes
made him the indispensable man in an exposed position but
which at other times brought him many a moment of regret,
is assuredly an integral part of his warm, vital personality.
This ability, together with his quick intelligence, his many
rich fields of interest, his fearlessness, and his abounding humor—all these qualities make him a source of inspiration to
others. His power to inspire us he demonstrated most often
when we were in consultation as to how some especially difficult problem was to be faced. Clear, brief, and pointed in questions and answers, he sees to it that the main issue is not side-
tracked. One also notices his ability to absorb new material in
an incredibly short time and to work with it effectively. I am
thinking of how he was able time after time to nonplus the
Germans with his knowledge of international law. Any one
who follows closely Berggrav's work during the critical years
of our Resistance struggles will be impressed with his warm
humanity, his intelligence, and—first and always—his urgent
desire to be useful in life.

These words express accurately Berggrav's whole
attitude during the War. We think of them in con-

nection with his negotiations for establishing the
Administrative Council, and also during the negotiations in June, 1940. Berggrav was active in the
matter until June 27, but he dropped out then
along with the Supreme Court and others because
he did not approve of the proposal that the King
be asked to abdicate. But always the Bishop's Office
was one of the strong centers of the growing Resistance movement. To it came the representatives
of the actors and athletes, who had been among the
first to be put under restraint. To it came pastors
and teachers. Here one dropped in to get advice
and the news. And here one came to put the final
touches to the pass-words that were to be sent out.

After September 25, Berggrav knew that there
would be a great struggle for the Church. He could
see in detail how it would come about; the enemy
would take the pastors, one by one, and drive them
from one point of resistance to another, each time
demanding some apparently trivial thing.

For instance, the parish papers were to be forced
to include items about the positive relationship between National Socialism and Christianity. Such
papers often printed items about this and that, why
not slip in this little article?

In this sort of thing, Berggrav was clear-sighted.
He knew that we must take a stand over one single
item, but it must be something that we felt bound

by conscience to fight for. So it was wise of him
not to make an issue of keeping the name of the
King in the prayers of the church. The prayers
for our countrymen in distant places remained.
And the King was prayed for in our churches during those years as never before. Berggrav knew that
the Germans were aware of the parallel situation in
1905, when the King's name was omitted from the
prayers of the Church by order of the Church
Department.

It was also typical of Berggrav that he entered
the fight on an issue that did not concern the
Church directly. His *Pastoral Letter* of January 15,
1941 was provoked by the attacks of Quisling's
Hird (combat force) and by the resignation of the
Supreme Court.

The Church could yield to a mandate that concerned herself. She could bear the shame of not allowing the King's name to be used in public worship, as long as no one was forbidden to pray
for the King individually. But the Church could
not keep silent when people suffered injustice and
when the judicial foundation of the nation was
wrecked, as it was when the Supreme Court was
deposed.

Berggrav had formulated his basic rules for the
Church's struggle from his observation of the strug-

gles of the German Confessional Church beginning
with the year 1933. He had even had a part in that
conflict. His article on "Arrested Pastors" from
Church and Culture, 1935, had been printed in German and circulated secretly in Germany.

Berggrav was constantly on the go during the
first year of the War. At first the prisoners of war
took much of his time, and he says that his contacts
with them furnished the principal light for him in
the dark spring of 1940. Later he was absorbed
with the political prisoners and with care for their
families. He collected money for the families of
the prisoners in an old cigar box in the vault at the
Bishop's office. He called it "Zarephath's cruse"*
for, like the widow of Zarephath's cruse, it was
never empty.

Did Berggrav do some reckless things in 1940?

Probably everybody did—that is, except for
those who did nothing at all. At any rate he took
no pains to be cautious. He could not bear to stand
guard over himself, although he received plenty of
friendly warnings.

But his lack of caution cost him many a dark
hour. One heavy shadow in the spring of 1940 was
the attack upon him over the London radio. Even
after the Liberation, there were some who revived

* Zarephath: I Kings 17:9ff.

these unjust accusations, in spite of the fact that
Berggrav had presented proof of their falsity in
the daily press and in *Church and Culture* in 1940
and later in his book, *When the Fight Came.*

CLIMAX IN THE STRUGGLE
OF THE CHURCH

The climax came on Easter Day, April 5, 1942,
when all the pastors laid down their office. By that
time Berggrav had been put out of the game and
was living under military guard in his cottage at
Asker. But it was he who had outlined all the plans.

The year 1941 had been spent in off-and-on
fencing, mostly of the defensive sort. For now the
State Department had made up its mind to con-
quer the Church. It tried by every means to re-
strict the power of the bishops and to entice or
threaten the pastors into coming over to its side.

Berggrav replied to all this activity from the
Department by issuing a circular from the bishops on December 15, 1941, entitled, "On the Order
of the Church."

Even now it is a pleasure to read this letter. In a
sense it is timeless. In its clear logic based on canoni-
cal law, it shows the correct relationship between

State and Church. It shows plainly that the independence of the Church and her bishops had its origin far back in the Norwegian Church: from earliest times all proposed changes or actions affecting the Church must be submitted first to the bishops for their recommendations. It is only through adherence to this practice that the relationship between Church and State has been maintained in Norway.

The thing that provoked the letter was merely a Departmental letter on the playing of the organ at Church services, but it had been sent to the pastors without having been submitted to the bishops. It had not aroused any special sensation. But Berggrav's circular in response ranks among the best things that he—with his assistants, of course—ever produced. And it came at exactly the right time. It gave the Church a last impulse of self-assurance before the final break came.

The breach had begun on February 1, with the infamous action of the State at Akershus (the old fort in Oslo) of installing Vidkun Quisling as prime minister of Norway. Captain Ola Fritzner had warned Berggrav of the impending event and had told him that the following days might be crucial ones for him and his family. They took advantage of the information, and Berggrav himself went into hiding in Lovisenberg Hospital, where he was supposed to be operated on for an ulcer and where he had to stay in bed on a milk diet.

The first important action of the State became, strangely enough, a furious attack on Berggrav by Terboven. The next day all the newspapers printed in facsimile a letter from Berggrav with an account of his attempts at making peace between Germany and England in the winter of 1939-1940. The letter had been found in the home of Ronald Fangen (a Norwegian Christian author) when he had been arrested a year and a half earlier.

It had not been used before, and was published now in order to destroy Berggrav's usefulness.

Terboven emphasized two things: Berggrav had said that he did not trust Hitler, and he had criticized England. The first charge was intended to call Hitler's wrath down upon him, the second to make him unpopular with the Jøssings. *Jøssing* was a nickname at first used by the Nazis for those who were opposed to Quisling; but it quickly became a name of honor among the Norwegians. It came from the episode at Jøssingfjord when the German ship *Altmark* with English prisoners of war aboard was forced into the fjord and the prisoners were set free. The action was a violation by Britain of the neutrality of Norway

Berggrav had long been fiercely attacked in the
Nazi press. But this present attack went beyond
bounds. Why was this letter being used now?

One reason certainly was that it was some sort
of retaliation for the fact that the State's action
in making Quisling prime minister had not worked
out as anticipated: Quisling was not chief in com-
mand over a Norway that had signed a treaty of
peace with Germany. But the principal reason was
that the Nazis wanted Berggrav out of the way.
They understood rightly that he was at the center
of the resistance of the Church, and now they
intended to render him harmless.

At any rate, Quisling's fury increased in the following weeks. Rightly or not, he believed that
Berggrav was the man who had upset his apple cart
in the present event and also at the time when the
Administrative Council had been organized.

It turned out, however, that it was Dean Fjellbu
at Trondheim and not Berggrav who first came into
the line of fire. At the time of the action at Akershus, a Nazi pastor had held a service at Nidaros
Cathedral, in spite of Fjellbu's protests. Fjellbu,
then, held a large special service at two o'clock of
the same day. Then the ground began to burn under
his feet.

Berggrav received a message by courier the next

morning, February 2, and immediately gave up the plans for his ulcer operation. Now he had to go out and operate himself, he said.

Not without reason! Things were happening fast. Fjellbu found himself in the Nazi's spotlight because of his special service. And then on February 5, the *Nasjonal Samling* (Norway's Nazi party) launched its Youth Service Organization, with its compulsory training in Naziism.

On February 14 came the Bishops' letter of protest against the youths' compulsory service. The protest was addressed to the Cabinet ministers, Skancke and Stang. The letter stated that it was the parents alone who were responsible for the training of their children and that the new organization would be something that countless parents would feel to be an intolerable influence on their children, something that might drive them to extreme action for the sake of their conscience.

The letter was swiftly circulated all through the country. In Berggrav's private office on the second floor of the Bishop's Residence, the mimeograph machine was working.

The letter was endorsed by all the Christian organizations, by the Lutheran Free Church, and by the Dissenters' Council. On February 28 there came a knock at Berggrav's door, and the Catholic Bishop of Oslo, Dr. Mangers, came in quietly. He asked if it would be possible for him to sign the Bishops' protest against the coercive law regarding children and young people.

"Yes, I would be happy to have you," Berggrav said. "Do you want to put it in writing?"

"Yes, I would prefer that."

"Be so kind as to sit down," Berggrav said, as he rose. "The Bishop of Oslo's chair is now vacant." He had already been suspended from office.

Mangers wrote a short statement, which was added to the stencil along with the protests from the other churches. There are not many other cases on record where a Catholic bishop has subscribed to a declaration drawn up by Protestants concerning a question of religious ethics. Mangers was later put to some annoyance by the Nazis, but he had no trouble from *Rome*.

In the midst of all this, Mrs. Berggrav was in a traffic accident and was seriously injured so that she was hospitalized for a long time. She was not discharged from the hospital until after Berggrav had been imprisoned.

Fjellbu's removal from office had come on February 20. Berggrav was told about it late that night in a telephone call from Bishop Krohn-Hansen in Tromsø. The latter believed that all the bishops should resign at once in protest.

Now Berggrav acted quickly. The Christian Joint

Council was summoned to a meeting the next morning at Hope's home, and the bishops' meeting was set for two days later.

Berggrav remembered two things. The first was what Supreme Court Justice Paal Berg had told him in December, 1941: "When the time has come for you, don't wait for Quisling to dismiss you. Take the offensive yourselves and lay down your offices. Your position will be stronger if you are active, not passive." The other recollection was of an interview with Bishop Otto Dibelius in Berlin in January, 1940. Dibelius had given up his office, but he declared that he would continue to work for the church, preaching and counseling, but not as a state official.

On the evening of February 23, all the bishops who had reached Oslo—those from Stavanger and Tromsø had not made it—gathered for a meeting with the members of the Christian Joint Council. There was no dissension among them, but the situation was grave. Before one o'clock the next afternoon, each bishop had written his own letter to the Church Department notifying it that he was laying down his office. Bishops Skagestad in Stavanger and Krone-Hansen in Tromsø were contacted by telephone, and Berggrav was able to advise the State Department that letters from them would be coming in the first mail.

Three principal points were made in the letters:

1. The State had deprived Dean Fjellbu of his rightful worship service.

2. The State had brought force and the police into the Church by trying to prevent Fjellbu from holding his special service.

3. The State had dismissed Fjellbu from office.

The letter closed with these words:

"The bishops of the Norwegian Church would be unfaithful to their call if they were to continue to cooperate with an administration which violates in this manner the rights of the congregation, adding injustice to violence—all without any valid ground according to the laws of the Church. I therefore hereby advise the Department that I am resigning the execution of my office. That is to say, whatever the State has committed to me, I surrender. The spiritual work and authority committed to me by my ordination at the altar of the Lord, are still mine with God, and rightly so. To be a preacher of the Word, the overseer of the congregation, and the counselor of the pastors, is and shall remain my call. I shall continue to fulfill these duties so far as it is possible for one who is not a state official. But to continue administrative cooperation with a State that uses force against the Church would be to break faith with the Holy of Holies.

"Like Luther we have tried to be loyal to the authorities so far as the Word of God and His commandments will permit it. But as the time came for Luther, so it has come for us to follow our convictions and to uphold the rightness of the Church as opposed to the injustice of the State. The forms of the State may change, but the Church knows, as her founding father knew, that God himself stands opposed to tyranny through the power of His Word and His Spirit. Woe unto us if we here do not obey God rather than man."

The letters came like a bomb to the table of the Cabinet member. The same afternoon, with the help of a relative of one of the bishops, he tried to persuade the bishops to recall their letters or at least to declare their loyalty to the State. There were threats of violence: the bishops would be contributing to Norway's becoming a protectorate; they would be held responsible for executions; thus they might be "responsible for the loss of at least a hundred innocent lives."

When these threats did not avail, the Church Department sent out telegrams that very evening, one to each bishop, informing him that his "request for dismissal" would be dealt with at the first Cabinet meeting and that until further notice he was suspended from office.

That term, "request for dismissal," was certainly misleading, but it was explained when the bishops'

letter was read in the Churches on the first of
March, together with a declaration of sympathy
from the pastors and parish councils. The pastors
wrote to the State Department, each declaring that
he still considered his suspended bishop the only
true bishop.

The first phase of the struggle was over. It was
strange for us pastors to meet Berggrav after he
had resigned his office while we continued in our
offices for another six weeks. We were summoned
one morning to a meeting in the Church for the
Deaf. It was filled with pastors when Berggrav
rose to thank those who had signed the declaration
that they still considered him their rightful bishop.
"It is to you that I wish to speak. If there is anyone here who has not made that declaration, I must
ask him to leave." An ominous silence followed as
Berggrav's eyes flashed over the pews. Nobody left.
They were all with him.

Then it came. "All of you who follow us bishops now must be prepared to run the greatest risks,
any kind of risk. Anyone among you who is not
prepared for anything might just as well leave
the ranks at once. It will be harder to withdraw
later. Each and everyone must know for himself
that he *wants* to take the risk involved."

He took out his pocket Testament and read
II Corinthians 6:1-10: "But as servants of the

Lord we commend ourselves in every way: through
great endurance, in afflictions, hardships, calamities,
beatings, imprisonments, tumults, labors, watching,
hunger, . . . in honor and dishonor, in ill repute
and good repute. We are treated as impostors and
yet are true; as unknown and yet well known; as
dying, and behold we live; as punished, and yet not
killed; as sorrowful, yet always rejoicing; as poor,
yet making many rich; as having nothing, and yet
possessing everything!"

The words were read slowly with great emphasis. Each syllable of this familiar passage took
on new meaning.

Berggrav did not have an easy time of it those
days. He was the only one who was given his dismissal in the first round. Hille's dismissal came a
week later and the other five the following week.
They were all obliged to report to the State Police
twice a day, and Berggrav had to move out of the
Bishop's residence.

The Nazi press blamed him for everything. He
was headlined in the newspapers more than anyone else. There were even some pastors who thought
that he had acted too quickly. Berggrav himself
was worn out, and his wife was seriously ill. Terboven's threats hung over his head. He had the feeling that it was hard to get everybody to go along
with him. There were some who thought that it

wasn't necessary to get so worked up just because the Dean had been dismissed. Couldn't Fjellbu have refrained from holding his special service?

Introspective as he was, all this troubled Berggrav. It might be well to emphasize here the fact that the real reason for the resignation of the bishops had not been the dismissal of Dean Fjellbu. That was the immediate occasion; but behind it was the great issue—the impressment of the young people. That imperiled the people. It was this that convinced the bishops that they must take up the fight at once.

So now Berggrav was a "private person," as Quisling's document of dismissal said. But he was never a better bishop than he was in the last six weeks of his freedom. He was deeply moved by the many expressions of sympathy and friendship from the pastors. He needed them.

On February 27 he was brought to the Palace for a dramatic "hearing." In the police car on the way, he took out his New Testament and read I Peter, chapter 3. Kristian Hansson, who had been with him when the police came, had suggested that he read the chapter. His eyes stopped at verse 14: "Have no fear of them, nor be troubled, but in your hearts reverence Christ as Lord."

He was reminded in the midst of his anxiety of the real purpose of it all. It was not the cause of

the Church nor Berggrav's personal cause that was
to be considered; it was Christ Himself. He considered the words as something of a judgment upon
him; he had been too much concerned with the
situation, with the fight. Now he saw matters in
a different light and prayed that Christ might be
hallowed within him—Christ and no one else. Then
he felt perfectly calm and went confidently up the
Palace steps to meet Quisling. The prime minister
sat at the head of the table, surrounded by Hagelin,
Fugelsang, Jonas Lie, Riisnæs, a few Nazi officials,
and two stenographers.

The "hearing" at first was concerned with his
part in establishing the Administrative Council
and the fall of the Quisling "government" in April,
1940. Quisling said outright that Berggrav was a
criminal who should have been beheaded a hundred
times. Even that would not have been enough. "But
we don't do such things," Quisling added.

Berggrav was questioned by all of them. He refused to give any information beyond the fact that
he had twice been brought before the German minister Bräuer. If they wanted to know more, they
would have to ask Bräuer. The first time he had
been taken by a German chauffeur, the second time
by two Norwegians.

Hagelin: Who were the two Norwegians?

Berggrav: I won't give their names. But they

were both members of the Nasjonal Samling. (They did not care to hear that!)

Jonas Lie: Do you remember what Bräuer said?

Berggrav: Very distinctly.

Jonas Lie: Did you take any notes on it?

Berggrav: Yes.

Lie: Are you willing to hand over the notes?

Berggrav: No.

Quisling: But you must have had some idea, some purpose. What were you thinking when you went along with this crime?

Berggrav: Thoughts are not subject to deposition. One has to answer only for one's words and deeds. By the way, Mr. Lie, you ought to know a little about this. For you sent me a letter in which you thanked me for my course of action after April 9.

This caused an explosion. Jonas Lie turned pale. The others roared with rage. It was Riisnæs who spoke first: This is insolence and audacity. You are a horrible Pharisee.

Berggrav (to Quisling): Mr. Minister President, perhaps we will get further if we omit abusive words? Won't the Minister President object to Riisnæs' expression?

Quisling (furiously): He is right. You are a criminal.

Berggrav (to Lie): But you surely remember that you wrote it?

Lie (sulky and angry): You turned out to be an entirely different person from what I thought.

Now for a while things were in such a turmoil that Berggrav could not manage to get them all down on paper in the right order. (Quisling had given him permission to take notes on the proceedings.) Jonas Lie and Hagelin went out for a while. Later it was discovered that they had gone out to arrange for a search of Berggrav's home in an attempt to find his notes on the interview with Bräuer. It was of course futile.

The second part of the questioning concerned the struggle with the Church. Berggrav asked a few questions as to why the bishops were treated so differently. Notes on this part of the hearing were sent by Berggrav to the other bishops at their secret addresses, as had become the practice.

"THE FOUNDATION OF THE CHURCH"

After all the bishops had been dismissed, there followed some scattered dismissals of pastors during the month of March. At the same time the opposition to the Youth Service was continuing. On March 10, three hundred teachers were arrested, and ten days later a thousand more—all of them because they had refused to join the "Teachers' Union." Most of them were taken to Kirkenes.

These developments caused many of the pastors about the country to think that the time had come to settle the score with the Nazis by a great proclamation to be followed by the resignation of all the pastors. Olav Valen-Sendstad came from Stavanger with a proposal for such a proclamation, and material for it was collected from all quarters. For in this settlement, or final denunciation, everything was to be included: the violations of justice, the encroachments upon the schools and churches, the compulsory training of young people.

On Sunday, March 22, the pastors read a kind of ultimatum from their pulpits, to the effect that if the views of the Church were not going to be respected, the pastors would not be able to continue in their office. In the afternoon of the same day, the Christian Joint Council started to work on the proclamation, which was to be entitled, "The Foundation of the Church." It was to present a comprehensive review of all that had happened, and to give the pastors some sort of standard to cling to for the future.

Berggrav worked all week on the first draft for this important document. Officially he was staying at the cottage at Asker, but since the police had removed his telephone, he had little opportunity for contact with others there. Then Cathrine and Nils Hals came to his assistance. They let him use the fireplace room in the basement of their home on Gyldenløve Street. They also let him use an office in town.

Saturday night, March 28, the Christian Joint Council was to have its final session on "The Foundation of the Church" at the home of Hallesby. At 1:30 in the morning their work was finally finished. They had been working since six o'clock. Now they were seated in silent prayer. Suddenly it struck Berggrav that something was wrong. The uneasiness grew within him, struggling against his sense of gratitude over the fact that the task was finished. Berggrav looked at Hallesby and said, "Are you completely satisfied with this?"

Hallesby hesitated and then replied, "No, now that you ask—"

Berggrav said, "Then we must discard the whole thing. We have to rewrite it!" It was clear to him now what was wrong. It had been written in the form of the old confessional writings, "We reject—" and "We believe—."

But he also saw that the tone was wrong. A good deal of their eagerness to fight had slipped in. So the men decided to meet again the next day at 1:30 in the afternoon. In the meantime Berggrav was to prepare a new draft without the belligerent spirit of the first one.

Berggrav then went "home" to the fireplace room

on Gyldenløve Street, got a couple of hours' sleep and then worked steadily until one o'clock. Some parts he left unchanged; the rest was rewritten in his unintelligible hieroglyphics.

The next day was Palm Sunday. The new draft was readily accepted. The mimeographing and circulation were left to Pastor Bonnevie-Svendsen. The officers of the Christian Council had agreed to accept the responsibility for the authorship, expecting to be arrested for it, as indeed they were.

Berggrav's part in "The Foundation of the Church" was finished. The declaration was read in the churches on Easter Day, and it was followed by the pastors' announcements that they too were resigning their office; and all this while Berggrav was sitting alone in his cottage thinking about what a "fateful day this was for the Church of Jesus Christ in Norway."

"The Foundation of the Church" is a good example of a church creed, or statement of faith, called forth by some crucial situation. At the same time there is something ageless about it. It is another development of the Christian's basic confession that Jesus Christ is Lord. One important aspect of this declaration is the emphasis put upon the total responsibility of the Church for human life.

It is true for most present-day ideologies—including even Naziism, Communism, and Liberalism—

that men can quite easily accept Christ as Savior, but they cannot accept Him as Lord. The Church may have an interest in eternal values, but she must not meddle in the problems of the times. That would be going back to medieval times with the Church the dominating force in politics.

To be sure the Church's power-politics of the Middle Ages is nothing to be imitated today. The alliance forged between Church and State under Constantine the Great had disastrous consequences. No one was able to find the right balance between the ecclesiastical and secular realms.

Luther tried to set this matter straight. It was important to him to show that the Church must not interfere in the domain of the State, as the popes had been doing.

But "The Foundation of the Church," while acknowledging Luther's distinction between the two realms, begins with the opposite problem. Now it was not the Church but the State that was threatening to become all-powerful. And so it was necessary in this confession to develop the significance of accepting Christ as *Lord*. This does not mean that the Church is to dominate the State, but that both Church and State must bow before God, and that the State has no right to interfere with the life of the Church.

The Declaration deals with this theme in six sections:

1. On the freedom of the Word of God
2. On the Church and Ordination
3. On the unity of the Church
4. On the rights and duties of parents, and on the place of the Church in the education of children
5. On the proper relationships between Christians and the Church with respect to the authorities of government
6. On the State Church

The whole document is of lasting worth. It should be included in textbooks on Christianity. At the same time, in the situation which brought it forth, it had explosive material, as for instance, the statement in Section 5: "Where the power of the State departs from the path of justice, the State is not an instrument of God, but a demonic power."

It was the quiet before the storm for Berggrav during Holy Week. He was to preach at the Cathedral, but not in vestments since he had been deprived of robe and collar.

While he was sitting in the cottage working on

his sermon on the afternoon of Holy Thursday, Kristian Hansson came with the message that the police had posted a decree prohibiting his preaching. The two men decided to go in to Oslo to find out what was going on. After they had left, a State policeman came to the cottage. When he learned that Berggrav had taken the train in to town, he started in pursuit by car, caught up with the train, found Berggrav in a compartment, and gave him the letter from the State Police that forbade him to appear at any gathering or even to leave his residence during Easter. Berggrav and the policeman went together to the office of the State Police, where the interdiction was confirmed. Berggrav was not even to go to church on Easter Sunday.

He asked for an hour for considering his situation—not because he was in doubt about what he was going to do—but in order to arrange certain matters before they came to pick him up, as he was sure they would.

After an hour he called up and said clearly to the police, "If you want to keep me from going to church, you will have to use force."

And so he spent the first of four Easter Sundays under police guard at the cottage. On Easter morning he wrote a long letter to his wife in Lovisenberg Hospital, saying among other things:

You know I am quite a cool fellow, but I woke up today with the one word *Christ* in my mind. And now that I have had my breakfast and have said hello to the new policeman, I sit down to write you, still feeling that it is Christ I want to write about. No one can describe or imagine His being. My belief is that He *is*. And He is *here*. In person. It seems to me that there is a shadow over His face. He is still suffering. Even after entering the Kingdom of God, this chord of pain still vibrates within Him. To me the fact of His resurrection stands forth more clearly than the actual cheers on that occasion. "It is finished." The words become the immovable pole of our existence. But it has its cost. The cost of living has not been abolished.

Easter Sunday afternoon the State Police came to bring him in for questioning. There was, of course, a great stir over the proclamation, "The Foundation of the Church," and over the resignation of the pastors.

In the brief questioning Berggrav admitted, according to the agreement made in the Council, that the Christian Joint Council was behind it all, and that he had written the draft of the document. But he said not a word about how it had been distributed.

Strangely enough he was taken back to the cottage, where a more rigorous watch was set up. He also had to submit to another unpleasant but fruitless search of his house. He was not arrested until two days later, when he was imprisoned at Bredtvedt. Kristian Hansson, Ingvald B. Carlsen, H. E.

Wisløff, and Ragnvald Indrebo were there already.
These men were released after ten days, but for
Berggrav it was the beginning of a three-year im-
prisonment. The others had been together, but
Berggrav was kept in solitary confinement.

During the first days at Bredtvedt, he wrote a
kind of diary which he managed to smuggle out
to his wife. It shows that he was dizzy, nauseated,
and somewhat despondent. But he made good use
of his experience as a prison chaplain. In his book,
The Prisoner's Soul and Ours, he had made the observation, "Prisoners become like children; they
develop a sensitive feeling for justice common to
those who are defenseless." He began to experience
this feeling. Some good friends had managed to get
a sleeping bag to him, and he enjoyed a good night's
sleep. But it was taken away from him, in accordance with the regulations. He became furiously
angry, and wanted to get hold of the inspector and
the director. Then suddenly he recognized the
"prisoner's soul" in himself. And he began to laugh.
It was typical of a prisoner to be upset over little
things.

It was during these days that he wrote his prison
song. It was sent to his wife. Later copies of it were
circulated all through the country. It was even
translated into English by an anonymous trans-
lator. This is the hymn:

SONG OF THE LONELY*

God, Thou art so close to me
   As I wait here all alone!
All about me speaks of Thee—
   Lattice window, walls of stone,
Whispering, like heaven above,
God, our Father, He is love.

Silence all about is deep
   But for guardsman's steps below.
Time itself is fast asleep,
   Deathly stilled each voice I know.
Then I lift my heart in prayer—
Loneliness finds heaven is there.

Longing for the ones most dear
   Burns like thirst within the soul;
Terror stealthily draws near;
   Memory winds her painful scroll.
Christ then heark'ning to my prayer
Fashions faith from dark despair.

From my friends come little gifts.
   These are Thine, which Thou hast sent;
Then my heart in gladness lifts
   Knowing well the greetings meant
Thou through friends' kind-heartedness
Would'st restore my cheerfulness.

I am under haughty power.
   Will they take my honor from me?
Has sin brought me to this hour?
   Was I all that I should be?
From my heart's perplexity
Christ's salvation sets me free.

---

* May be sung to the melody of "Jesus Christ, My Sure Defense."

All I have—futility!
　Doubtful futures Thou wilt clear;
From my loss bring victory
　When I yield Thee all things here;
From life's pressure, then release,
Daily blest with faith and peace!

At first the Nazis planned to have Berggrav tried
on the charge of having given false testimony before the Court (Paragraph 166 of the Penal Law).
It would be based on the notorious hearing at the
palace on February 27. A rather imperfect report
of the hearing had come over the London radio.
When he was questioned again on March 25, Berggrav had been asked how this story could have
found its way to London. He admitted having
mentioned the matter to friends, but denied having made a written report of it. He had, however,
he explained, mentioned the last part of the hearing,
about the Church's resistance, in a letter to the
bishops, but to no one else.*

Unfortunately, the state policeman who questioned Berggrav on March 25 had a letter in his
desk drawer in which the hearing was mentioned;
and this letter was addressed in Berggrav's own
handwriting, not to one of the bishops, but to Sexton Weisser at Kristiansand. Berggrav did not know
about it until some time after the questioning.

---

*These notes, which have been referred to before on page 154, were not
written out in full until after March 31, that is, after this questioning.

Yet he had told the truth, and he could prove it. Sexton Weisser's was the undercover address for Bishop Maroni, and Berggrav did not feel that he was obliged to disclose these innocent secret addresses. But now he was to be tried for giving false testimony.

It did not work out that way after all. A counsel was appointed for Berggrav who, in spite of being a member of the Nazi party, turned out to be a fine fellow. Skillfully and boldly he picked the accusation to pieces. For one thing, it was entirely wrong for a policeman not to exhibit the evidence he had in his possession. The judges in the so-called People's Court agreed with the defense. But the story that Berggrav was a liar was broadcast through the Nazi press, and of course spread even farther.

There were many signs to indicate that Quisling had intended to go much farther in his campaign against Berggrav. The "Foundation of the Church" was to be branded a document of insurrection and the resignations of Church offices as action inimical to the State; then Berggrav was to be shot after a hasty trial. The expressions Quisling used in his articles all point to such a plan: Berggrav was "an impostor and a traitor"; and "by their behavior they force us to destroy them." In a threatening letter to all the pastors who had resigned their posi-

tions, it was said that their action "would be dealt
with as an act of insurrection directed against Norway's freedom and independence." And again, "In
the next few days things will happen that should
be of the utmost significance to each one of you
in the stand you have taken."

One of the threatened happenings was probably
to have been the execution of Berggrav. But the
Germans would not permit it. Himmler sent a telegram to Terboven, asking, "Why is Berggrav in
prison?" The telegram itself was enough to put a
stop to Quisling's plans. It was sent because the
Norwegian Home Front had contact with the
Germans through Lieutenant Colonel Th. Stelzer.
The latter had arranged with Count von Moltke, a
member of Admiral Canari's espionage staff, to
telegraph immediately if Berggrav was arrested.
When Moltke received the message, he at once informed the highest authorities in Berlin. Berggrav
knew Himmler. He had had a long interview with
the German at the time he was taken to Skaugum
to explain his Pastoral letter to Terboven and
Himmler.*

It seems quite certain that things would have
gone differently if the Germans had not interfered.
Von Moltke himself came to Oslo on behalf of the

---

* There is an account of this interview in *When the Fight Came,* pp.
166-186.

German military intelligence service *(Abwehr.)* He was a good Christian and was close to the group that later tried to assassinate Hitler. He was alarmed at the stupidities of Quisling, and he reported the fact that the whole conflict with the Church endangered Germany's military security in Norway.*

On Monday, April 13, the trial of Berggrav was to begin in the People's Court. But nothing happened. On April 16 the warden came with the word that Berggrav was to be freed.

His joy was great. There was a car waiting at the gate. He was happy that he was going to have a ride into town. And he got it! Three uniformed officers came out and told him that they had orders to take him away. In the car was another surprise, for there was his son Øivind Seip Berggrav. Øivind informed his father, "We are both prisoners. We are to be interned in the cottage at Asker." The young man had been his father's secretary at the bishop's office for the past two years.

So off to the cottage! There Berggrav found their

---

* I had some personal contacts with certain of his men who were gathering information. When I told one of them that the pastors were threatened with having to move from their parishes if they did not recall their resignations, the man replied ironically, "That is excellent. Just take your wife and children along, and travel the roads with a handcart. Hold meetings every evening. I am sure that if Norway's 1,000 pastors set out that way, the men in Berlin will understand fast enough how foolish this whole business is."

maid, Rikke Henriksen,* and twelve armed policemen, who were to guard these three.

Here Berggrav stayed for three years to the day.
His two companions were released the first summer. He was never given any explanation as to how
it happened that he was free one moment and interned the next. It was a compromise. Quisling had
persuaded the Germans to let him go so far, but
no farther.

IMPRISONMENT AT THE COTTAGE, 1942-1945

The instructions for guarding Berggrav were
worked out at the Oslo Police Presidium. The paper,
which bore the heading "Instructions for Police
Guard at Granstua (Spruce Cottage)," consisted of
13 paragraphs. The worst stipulation was that the
watch was under the supervision of the Criminal
Police Force in Oslo, and that there were to be frequent inspections at irregular intervals by the
commander of the Criminal Force personally and
also by the Gestapo.

These controls from Oslo put a strain on the
nerves for three long years. Inspection came at the
most unexpected times, and often not by the reg-

---

* The family housekeeper for many years, who looked after Berggrav
faithfully until his death.

ular road up to the cottage. Suddenly policemen
would come bursting out of the spruce forest behind the house. There was no way to guard against
such surprises.

The watch consisted of 12 armed guards, with
three men on duty at all times, walking around
the house. The cottage was to be kept locked, and
only the chief guard was to have a key. He lived
in the house, in the room next to Berggrav's. The
other guards were quartered in a neighboring cottage which had been seized for this use.

Paragraph 7 of the instructions stated categori-
cally: "All visiting is prohibited." No exceptions
were made. Even Berggrav's wife was not permit-
ted to visit him, despite her repeated applications
for permission.

Paragraph 6 read, "The team of guards must
not enter into conversation with Dr. Berggrav.
All requests are to be referred to the guard commander." This meant that for three years Berggrav was not supposed to speak to a living being
except the chief guard. His son and the maid had
soon been released. His son became ill the latter part
of July and was transferred to the prison hospital
(Oslo Municipal Hospital) at Ullevål. He was
freed a little later. Berggrav thought that it was
unreasonable for the maid to have to stay there
just to keep house for him, so he petitioned to have

her released. This petition was granted. But when
Mrs. Berggrav, after her discharge from the hospital, applied for permission to join her husband in
his imprisonment, the application was not even
answered.

Paragraph 10 read, "Dr. Berggrav is allowed to
move about outside at certain times during the day,
but only in the area shown by the red lines on the
map (immediately around the house). The chief
guard is then to watch him the whole time, and
two of the guards are to be alerted." They were
told not to be more than three feet away from him.

So strict were the regulations that had to be
checked whenever the sudden inspection came!
That meant that there was always a risk if one
broke them. There were times when the rules had
to be followed to the letter, when for one reason
or another there was an "alert."

Of course Berggrav did everything he could to
ease the situation. He was especially good at getting along with the guards. A Swedish newspaper,
foolishly enough, made the statement that Berggrav converted all his guards. The immediate result was that the best guards were replaced. Later
no guards stayed there very long.

Still the watch became gradually easier. The Oslo
Police replaced the State Police; and it was not
possible to provide a sufficient number of Nazi

policemen. Some were actively friendly and took
great risks for Berggrav's sake; others were only
more relaxed in their duties, closing their eyes to
what was going on. But all of them broke the
regulation that they were not to talk to him.

One of the first things Berggrav did was to get
himself an extra key so that he could move around
a bit on the property while the guards sat in the
sun and played cards on the other side of the house.

But Berggrav was not satisfied with this. His
first real excursion came from a pure and simple yearning for freedom. Late in July of 1942
he wanted to take a trip to the top of Vardåsen to
watch the sunrise. He crawled out of the kitchen
window late one evening while the guards were
busy on the other side of the house. He got into a
sleeping bag in the woods a little way from the cottage and watched the stars until it began to get
light. Then he walked to the top of Vardåsen.
There he saw the sun rise in the northeast over Oslo.
He even made himself some coffee. At six o'clock
in the morning he walked down again and waited
with his heart in his throat until he could manage
to slip in again. It was a marvelous experience, quite
unnecessary and quite typical of Berggrav.

Later on he became bolder, especially after he
had a police uniform made for himself. One of the
sympathetic guards helped him. He kept the uni-

form in the closet of the room of the chief of the guards. There were two chiefs, one on duty for a week at a time. Each guard thought that the extra suit belonged to the other guard.

The uniform was really for Berggrav to use at the end of the war in case the "Hird" attempted a personal attack on him. He had been warned that his name was on the list of hostages who were to be shot in case anything happened. In such an emergency he would put on the uniform, mingle with the guards, and disappear.

But it would also give him an excellent disguise if he wanted to take a trip to Oslo. Altogether he made four trips to Oslo in the three years, each time on an especially important mission. There were people he *had* to meet, and he held his rendezvous in the "fireplace," the undercover name for his haunt at Hals's on Gyldenløve Street.

A small mustache which he glued on and a pair of glasses completed his disguise. No one could recognize him.

I discovered this fact when I visited him at the cottage. While he was there, he had several secret visitors. I had been at Grini, the German concentration camp near Oslo, for several weeks. Then the message came from Berggrav: I must meet him. He wanted to know how it was faring with Hope and Hallesby. They had also ended up at Grini.

I received exact instructions on a typewritten slip—a train at such and such a time to Asker, the main road toward Drammen, the first road to the left, and so on. At a certain spot I was to take a right-angle turn and walk straight into the woods for 50 yards. I went, counting the steps . . . 48, 49, 50, and stood looking around. Then Berggrav, with a smile, popped out from behind a bush. He wore an old pair of trousers and an old jacket. "Follow me," was all he said.

Then I was smuggled into the cottage and up to his room, which was overflowing with manuscripts. First Berggrav had to go down to make some coffee. He put a long dissertation into my hand for me to read while he was about it. I was soon completely absorbed in this excellent paper proposing a revision of the service book of the Church. I was just beginning to smell the coffee when the door opened suddenly and a furious voice asked, "What are you doing here?"

In front of me stood a fuming policeman. "Where is the Bishop? You know where he has fled. Out with it, at once! We have the means to make you confess!"

I was speechless. I had no excuses; and I began to set my house in order.

Then off came the "officer's" cap, off came the glasses, off came the mustache—and there was Berg-

grav. I don't believe I laughed so hard at any other
time during the whole war as I did then. Berggrav
had to hush me up. It might be dangerous for the
chief guard, who, by the way, was out on a little
trip. As if anything more could put a scare in me!

We had a fabulous evening. Berggrav had all the
news. He was better informed than I. He did not
tell me then, however, that he had a radio, too. But
I thought he was suspiciously well-informed about
London news. The radio was kept in a scrub pail
in the kitchen. At night it was carried up into
the woods.

Berggrav had a few other visitors, too; principally his wife. He thought that it was relatively
safe for her to come, for none of the guards ever
came into his bedroom. He managed her visits in
this way: One dark night near the beginning of his
imprisonment, he quietly opened a window and
threw some logs into the woods, hurling them with
all his might. Naturally the sounds caused a com-
motion, for the guards thought that the Bishop
had escaped. The chief guard himself rushed out.
No one discovered anything, but the hubbub was
great.

When the chief guard came up the stairs again,
Berggrav was standing in a long white nightshirt
at the topmost step to give him a rough talking to.
Wasn't it enough that they kept him locked up?

Now they were going to deprive him of his much needed night's rest? Was there no limit? Didn't they feel sure that twelve men and a chief guard could watch over one old man? And so on.

As a result, the chief guard promised upon his faith and honor never again to disturb him at night. And that I can understand, for when Berggrav pretended to be angry, he looked dangerous. Whether he was in a nightshirt or a police uniform! So Berggrav could feel relatively safe in his room.

Toward the end of his imprisonment, he gave up using the police uniform, relying principally on the mustache. One New Year's Eve he unexpectedly showed up at his son's place at Blommenholm, where the whole family was gathered. He posed as a Swedish engineer, and even his son was fooled for a while.

His neighbors helped him a great deal. At two of the cottages he could receive visitors, if necessary, and in one house nearby his sixtieth birthday was celebrated on October 25, 1944. There he was presented with a bound book containing handwritten greetings from many of his friends.

But one must not think from all this that Berggrav's prison term was one long series of escapades. The episodes just related were exceptions to the usual order. Most of the time he was all alone, and there were long stretches when he could not take any liberties at all. It depended largely on who the guards were, and especially on what kind of chief guard was on duty. Not all of them were sympathetic; and even though most of them were won over to him, neither he nor they dared risk chances with the inspection. It came often and irregularly, occasionally when he had visitors from outside. He succeeded in smuggling them out, but only by a hair's breadth, and the strain was great.

Worst of all was the loneliness through three long years. Fond of fellowship as he was, he suffered greatly from lack of daily contact with persons he could talk to. It is not easy for a man of his temperament to have no outlet.

He overcame the hardships by living a strictly disciplined life. He functioned like a clock, dividing the day carefully—so much time for sleep, so much for physical work, and so much for writing. He became an excellent cook and never skipped either dinner or shaving—"to keep my self-respect," he said.

His day went like this: up at 7:30, breakfast and reading; outdoor work from 10 to 11; writing till noon; lunch at 12:30; an hour in bed before dinner, followed by relaxing exercises. He always changed clothes for his dinner at 5:00. Then came coffee and more writing. He went to bed at 10:00, with some time for reading in bed.

His outside work consisted of chopping wood in winter and gardening in summer. When the Liberation came, fourteen cords of dry firewood stood nicely stacked in the yard; and he had kept himself supplied with firewood all the time. He felled the trees and cut them up himself. In the summer he scraped the earth from the cracks in the rocks and made a strawberry patch. The third summer, he harvested about 25 pounds of berries.

His writing comprised, first of all, the seven books that he finished and published after the war. They were, in the order that he worked on them, *Norwegian Church Profiles, Times and Texts* (the proposal for revising the service book of the Church), *Humor and Gravity, The Soul of the Child and Religion, Man and State, The Order of the Church in Norway,* and *When the War Came.* His book on the order of the Church contains his first proposals of regulations which would give the Church more freedom from the State.

Besides these books, there are several unprinted works, primarily the interesting memoirs of his childhood and youth. His weekly letters to his wife were also significant. They had to be sent through the State Police, and Mrs. Berggrav usually had to go to the office of "Major General" Marthinsen to read them there. They were not given to her. But Berggrav had made copies of them; and they are remarkable reading. There was no sense in writing about private affairs. Such letters were forwarded differently. These weekly letters are short essays on everything under the sun: art, nature, psychology, literature. He was able to get the books he wanted to have, and he read a great deal which he later commented on in his letters.

He did some writing that involved considerable risk. He continued to be used as an advisor for the Home Front, especially when any difficult problem arose. He helped not only with advice on their action during the war, but also with plans for the transition period [after the war] and for the judicial settlement with the Nazis.

The book most fraught with danger was *Man and State*. He dedicated it to "Paal Berg, Chief Justice of Norway's Supreme Court, in gratitude for the good done in evil times." There is no doubt as to what the *good* was that the Court and the Church experienced in their working together: It was the powerful hold of *justice* over the Norwegian mind and conscience. Berggrav shows that only a sense of the sacredness of justice can prevent the State from coming under demonic control. He presents an historical survey of the role justice has played in the State from Plato through Machiavelli, Thomas Hobbes, and Hugo Grotius, up to the

democratic States of modern times and their struggles against dictatorship.

Today we are most interested in Berggrav's discussion of the dangers threatening our democracies.
Like the leaders of the People's High School movement, he advocates information about politics. "If
we are to begin again in the true democratic way,
we must *go back to the people,* and then forward
for mankind, whatever the cost; forward for human rights and for the convictions upon which
they are based. Election laws must do more than
satisfy the mathematical requirements of the 'Party.' There must be provision for getting acquainted
with political personalities and for direct contacts
between the voter and his representatives in government. Unless this happens, the individual man will
lose and the machines of power will win." (See
p. 155, *State and Man.*)

The book contains, as supplementary material,
Berggrav's address at the Jurists' Association (February 5, 1942) on "Religion and Right," and also
the address on Luther that he delivered at a number
of pastors' meetings in 1941. In the latter address
he emphasized a modern tendency to quote Luther
out of context: "Lately we are often asked to consider what Luther has to say about the two realms
[Church and State]. Out of its context, this is a

confusing statement. It is time to set the matter straight: To Luther as to us there is *only one realm,* the realm of God."

Unfortunately, *Man and State* has received too little attention in the political discussions of our post-war times. It contains some enlightening accounts of the experiences of the Home Front, which might well be passed on to our present-day politicians. It is presented soberly and written from intimate knowledge of the heights the Norwegian people can rise to for common political good. All persons and parties need to hear about the contributions made by the Church to the political wellbeing of the nation.

ESCAPE

In view of how lax the guards were, Berggrav might have escaped any time. And he was urged to do so many times. On Christmas Eve in 1942 some of the Home Front men had planned to kidnap him and send him to Sweden. But the man at the head of the scheme was arrested for other reasons, and the plan had to be dropped. Berggrav did not know anything about it until afterwards.

Later another group got in touch with Berggrav through his family. But Berggrav refused to make the attempt. The principal motive behind such schemes was the Bishop's safety. He was believed to be on the list of hostages who were to be shot in any emergency. There was also, no doubt, a desire to flout Quisling *(å gi Quisling "en nese")*, and at the same time to encourage the Resistance Movement.

Berggrav realized himself that there was considerable risk in being Quisling's prisoner; on the other hand there was the danger that others would be taken as hostages if he escaped. Above all he felt that his place was in Norway.

Another factor to be considered was the risk that the Bishop's situation would become especially critical in the final phase of the war. As early as 1943 Berggrav talked over this possibility with one of the "good" chief guards. He agreed that the Bishop might be in grave danger at that time. In the last desperate struggle the usurpers of the government would try to get hold of Berggrav's person in order to have a good card in their hands. Berggrav rather early made up his mind to escape when the war seemed to be drawing to a close.

During the first days of April, 1945, the end seemed to be in sight. Berggrav asked a trusted guard for advice. He received an unconditional answer: He must make his escape before the collapse of Germany was complete. How was it to be arranged? The guards were held personally responsible for Berggrav and they would certainly be in trouble

if it was found that they had not guarded him
properly.

Then Berggrav proposed a plan. First of all, the
guards were to tighten their watch. They were
being changed constantly, for Quisling feared that
they would come under the Bishop's influence.
Now, Berggrav said, they must follow the rules to
the letter, so that after the escape there would not
be the slightest evidence that the guards had been
lax in their watch.

Then the guards must be subjected to a real attack, but without any shooting. The chief guard
must be bound hand and foot; and nothing should
be discovered until the time for the guards to be
relieved.

Berggrav made all the arrangements with the
"assailants." One of the neighbors saw to it that
the Military Organization (of the Home Front)
at Asker undertook the job, and Berggrav discussed
all the details with the leaders at a meeting at a
neighbor's home. There was a Mil. Org. man from
Oslo there also. Berggrav assumed that he would
let his contacts know about the plan.

The Bishop chose the date—the night of April
16-17, when he knew he would have trustworthy
guards. On the afternoon of the 16th he spoke
plainly to the guards who had the watch from three
to six o'clock. They were the ones who would have

the watch from midnight on. They agreed to the plan, but they were not told that the chief guard was also in the game.

Then Berggrav calmly packed his knapsack, and at 8:30 in the evening he crept out of the house and into the woods. He walked calmly, quietly down to Asker station, with his oldest son a few yards behind him. He took the train to Skarpsno [the last stop before the Oslo terminal], where he was met by the Swedish vice consul, who took him in his diplomat's car to a hiding place on Dunker Street. Kathrine Berggrav was sitting there waiting for him. She had made all the arrangements in Oslo, and had gone into hiding with the whole family.

It was a wonderful evening. Berggrav told them just what was going to happen next. And it all did go exactly according to plan.

At 12:30 A.M. some men came out of the woods at Asker, shouting, "Can anyone here tell us the way to the station?" The guards went over to the fence. Then the flashlights came on, and the orders, "Hands up!" The guards were securely bound and gagged. But first their uniforms were torn to indicate that there had been a real fight. They were laid in the woods, in the exact spot that Berggrav had chosen for them, where the ground was good and dry.

Then came the turn of the chief guard in the

cottage. A ladder was set up against the window of Berggrav's room, where there was a light. From there the "liberators" proceeded to the next room, where the chief guard was "taken by surprise"! He was bound securely with English parachute lines, to give the impression that Berggrav had been liberated by specialists from outside. The guard had to remind the men to gag him, for they had almost forgotten that in their haste. Then they left. The whole thing had taken three quarters of an hour.

The escape in all its details was not so simple as it sounds. The cottage where all the other guards were sleeping was not far away. And there was still the chance of a night-inspection. And so a complete Home Front unit was along, fully armed in case anything unexpected happened. They had kept the whole area under watch from early morning of the 16th and were a little uneasy because six Gestapo men had come up the road in the forenoon and had disappeared into the woods. They were not reported to have returned, so the men had to reckon with this element of uncertainty. But everyone did an excellent job, and all came off exactly as planned.

At the change of guard at three in the morning, everything was discovered. The first thing the fresh guards saw was the ladder up to Berggrav's window. Then they discovered the empty bed. The men rushed into the chief guard's room and found him bound and gagged in bed, but safe and sound. Later the other guards were found, and the big alarm went out. At five in the morning the State Police and the Gestapo came with cars and police dogs. Shortly afterward the following telegram went out from the Oslo Police Office:

To the Chiefs of Police at all stations:

During the night armed men freed Dr. Eivind Berggrav from his place of internment at Asker by overpowering the crew of guards. Please take up search.

Commander, Criminal Dept.

Berggrav in his place of hiding was kept informed about the progress of the search. His oldest son came the next evening with a report which the Home Front had intercepted by listening in on the telephone line of the State Police shortly after noon on April 17. The report said that "Berggrav had been abducted by members of the Home Front at 12:30 a.m." There followed a long description of the assault, with the conclusion that "This assault was so well planned that the guards would have been powerless even if there had been double the number armed with machine guns. The guards were attacked; they lay bound and gagged until 3:30 a.m., when the relief guards came on duty. By that time the whole attacking force was well on its way to the border. The telephone line had been cut."

The report brought great relief to Berggrav, for
the guards apparently were not to be accused. Confirmation came the next evening when his son
brought in copies of the evidence given by all the
guards to the Gestapo. They were all released within
24 hours. Everything had turned out just right except for one point: The top leaders of the Home
Front were mystified. Berggrav believed that they
had been informed; but the organization was of
necessity so decentralized that it took time before
a report could get from one group to the next. As
a result, some of the leaders of the Home Front
feared that the "kidnappers" might not have been
Home Front men, but Nazis or Communists.

Fortunately the matter was soon cleared up so
far as the Front men were concerned; but the mis-
understanding gave the Communists the opportunity to fish in troubled waters. In their illicit
publication, *Radio News,* for April 24 they carried
this story:

The liberation of Bishop Berggrav has created some confusion within certain civilian sections of the Home Front. However, we can now lift the veil a little to report that he is in
our hands. He is being well cared for and, of course, will not
be subjected to any ill treatment by us. We were forced to
take this step, because it had been reported to us that the
Bishop, after such a long period of isolation under the con-
stant pressure of Nazi propaganda, had begun to show Nazi
sympathies—quite a natural possibility, of course. But what
a scandal it would have been if the Bishop, under pressure

from the Nazis had come forward and professed his belief in Naziism! Until further notice we intend to take care of him in a better way. He begs us to greet his friends and to say that his belief in victory is again unshaken.

Some time earlier the Communists had objected in another of their illicit publications to Berggrav's endangering Norwegian lives in order to bring "his sanatorium stay to an end."

These illicit newspapers were widely circulated. Communists attached great importance to their papers and received some help for them from the leaders of the Home Front. These two statements about Berggrav created some uncertainty among the people and were also a forewarning of later Communist attacks on him.

Now Radio London announced that "the communique regarding Bishop Berggrav was unfortunately all wrong." And the next day Göteborg's *Trade and Navigation Newspaper* came out with a telegram from London to the effect that people there believed that it was either the free Norwegian Home Forces or else Quisling who had kidnapped Berggrav.

About the same time announcements appeared in all the Oslo papers to the effect that the State Police were offering a reward of 10,000 Norwegian kroner for information that would lead to a solution of the case. This announcement said, reasonably enough after what the Communists had printed, that Berggrav had been seized by some Communist group.

Then rumors came out that he was in Sweden where several people reported having seen him. Berggrav felt that this rumor was fortunate for him and that it might settle the case. He then had a message sent to Bishop Aulén with the request that the Swedish Radio report that Bishop Aulén knew Berggrav was in safe hands, thus giving the impression that he was in Sweden. The announcement was made, but too late. It came over the Swedish Radio on May 7, the day that the flags went up in Norway signifying the end of the War in Europe. But the confusion about Berggrav continued. Rumors went from person to person, wondering what Berggrav could possibly be thinking of doing now. These rumors were Communist-inspired. Berggrav himself and the few others who really knew had to keep quiet. For it must not be discovered at any cost that the guards had had anything to do with the escape, or it would be all up with them. So Berggrav, for the sake of the guards, disregarded himself.

I had had one contact with Berggrav on April 29. I had held a morning service at Uranienborg Church. My wife was sitting next to a country teacher, as she thought, who sang all the hymns with a powerful voice. He remained seated all through the long communion service and the later baptismal service; and she thought he was a peculiar person. When she finally met me outside of the church, the "teacher" came over to us. "Good morning and God's peace to you! I am Berggrav, but keep still about it!"

No one could have recognized him, at least not from the front, for glasses and a mustache made him a different man. But from the back, the nape of his neck and his ears looked familiar, and I was a little uneasy as we walked up to Dunkers Street. By this time contacts had been made openly with the leaders of the Home Front. The next day he had a long interview with Paal Berg, and soon he took his place with the others. He had been with them from the beginning in 1940-1941, when Gunnar Jahn, Paal Berg, he, and others had formed the "Inner Circle" which was the forerunner of the leaders of the Home Front.

When the telegram to ring the bells in all the churches was sent out on May 7, he came out in the open and signed the telegram together with the chairman of the Provisional Directors of the Church, Johannes Ø. Dietrichson.

LIBERATION

For Berggrav himself the spring and summer of 1945 was a difficult period. In the midst of their rejoicing over their liberation some people still found time to denounce Berggrav. And besides that, the Bishop had personal worries. His youngest son, who had been the head courier for his father at the cottage, had been arrested for other reasons by the Gestapo before Christmas in 1944, and he had become ill from the treatment he had received. Fortunately, he recovered fairly quickly, but it was a heavy burden for the Bishop for some time.

What was hardest of all on Berggrav was that the falsehoods circulated about him were hurting the Church. Some were following the practice of blackening the man to hurt the cause. Many did not realize what was going on; but some within the Church let themselves be deceived into thinking that there was something wrong with Berggrav.

The attacks centered mainly about two things: his activities in 1940 and his attitude toward the principle of justice applied in dealing with the Nazis and those who had cooperated with the Germans.

Even in 1940 Berggrav had explained the controversial situation that arose in April of that year. He had sent reports to the newspapers and had let all the papers and documents regarding the situation be printed in *Church and Culture*. It was clearly evident that his trip to the Krokskogen was not an attempt to persuade the Norwegian soldiers to surrender, but to help rescue Norwegian civilians who had been surrounded up there and who were

about to be shot by the Germans. My sister, Dr.
Gunhild Johnson, went up there on Saturday, April
13, as far as Ringerike, in the service of the Red
Cross. Any attempt for her group to get through
the lines was blocked, but Gunhild had seen a
group of civilians being led away by the Germans.
In answer to her questions, she was told that they
were to be shot because they had used weapons
without being in uniform. When she returned to
Oslo, she told me about it, and together we went
to the Bishop's residence Sunday morning to ask
Berggrav to do something about it. He had received
similar requests from other quarters and felt obliged
to see what he could do.

He set out the next day. The Germans followed
him part of the way; but up in the hills to Stub-
dal he was alone except for some Norwegian policemen who verified his story of what happened. He
had an electric loudspeaker with him, one that the
police had furnished. He shouted through it into
the woods, "This is the Norwegian Red Cross. If
there are any Norwegian boys that need help or
advice, speak up!" Out of the woods came a uniformed Norwegian ski-patrol, with whom they
talked. Berggrav told them what he knew about the
German posts and forces; and the leader of the
ski-patrol, Torolf Prytz, reported that everything
was all right on the Norwegian side.

Down in the village the Germans had taken a picture of Berggrav while he was trying out the loudspeaker before he and the policemen had gone on alone. The Germans put this photograph on the cover of their big magazine *Signal* with the caption, "The Norwegian Bishop Berggrav appeals to the Norwegian troops to give up their useless resistance against the Germans."

Berggrav had *Signal* seized, sent his account of the incident to all the newspapers, and also had the story come out in *Church and Culture* in the summer of 1940. Nevertheless, the whole lie was repeated in June 1945 in the Communist paper, *Freedom*. The author of the article showed that he knew about Berggrav's refutation of the charge in *Church and Culture* by quoting from it in another connection! In 1945, *Freedom* was a large paper, a successor of the illicit Communist paper of the same name.

Other charges were being made against Berggrav also. On June 26, *Freedom* came out with an editorial headed, "The Church to be Mobilized for Reaction." It quoted a circular letter from Berggrav to his pastors written October 23, 1940. He was advising them about what to do if a declaration of loyalty to the Nazis should be required of them. In conclusion the letter said, "A third anxiety has arisen as to whether one should join the *Nasjonal*

Samling. Everyone must act in accordance with his own convictions on this point. No one can or must allow himself to be *driven* by any other consideration."

This gave the paper the opportunity to claim that Berggrav had said it was all right for anyone to join the Nazis if it was in accordance with his own convictions! As if we pastors had not understood what he meant. For it was only the Nazis that would "drive" a man to act against his convictions at that time!

Berggrav was also attacked for trying to make peace with the Germans on June 17, 1940. It is true that he took part in the negotiations and that he formulated the proposal. But the point is that *his proposal never was presented.* It served as a basis for discussion for the Norwegians before negotiations were broken off. But Berggrav was one of those who dropped out because he was not willing to go along with those who wanted the King to abdicate.

And then there were attacks against Berggrav because of his views on the final judgment of the war criminals. During his internment he had written a long article on the *People's Judgment of the Nasjonal Samling.*

A great cry for vengeance against the Nazis had gone up all over the country. Berggrav had been asked to furnish a kind of ideological basis of judgment so that the final sentences would be the work of *justice*, not of *power*. It was emphasized that the public must be told that the Court would be stern, so that men would not try to take justice into their own hands. This was indeed a dangerous assignment to carry out, but Berggrav did not want to refuse to do it.

When it appeared, the article was subjected to attacks from every quarter. For one thing, Berggrav had come out openly in opposition to capital punishment, and therefore some thought his proposals were much too *mild*. Others objected to the second part of the article in which the Bishop discussed various ways of winning the guilty ones back into society. He submitted a detailed proposal for later revision of the sentences of those convicted, with extensive access to mercy—a proposal that by and large was followed after some years had passed. But to begin with it raised a storm of protest. Berggrav was nicknamed the "silken Bishop" in an editorial in one of the papers, and at that moment no one wanted to hear about any kind of "silk front." And there were many who thought ill of Berggrav's request for mercy for Quisling.

Later, attacks from another quarter became stronger. All those who had become members of the Nazi Party in Norway found it hard to swallow the fact that Berggrav held all party members equally guilty. His article stressed the fact that the struggle in Norway was actually a fight for or against Naziism. The King, the Supreme Court, the Church, and the schools—these had taken an active stand against Naziism. Thus, Berggrav held, everyone must see that in this issue the "first commandment of the catechism of the nation" was at stake. And for the sake of the future, it must be made clear that during the war membership in *Nasjonal Samling* was against the law.

But once the Law had spoken, even if it meted out only symbolic punishment, that should be the end of the matter. Then the time had come to forget it all.

Today the war trials are forgotten by almost everyone. No one thinks any more about whether a man was a member of the N. S. or not. I wonder if this would be true if we had not followed the course outlined in *The People's Judgment*. Now the former Jøssings know that their former foes have had their punishment and that the matter is settled once and for all. In spite of all the bitterness at the time, the trials turned out better than anyone could have expected in 1945. And in my opinion, our thanks are due to Berggrav, whose clean, stern writing with its long perspective helped show us the way. Those who think that the whole article was too harsh should reread it, carefully. The last half of it deals with the principle by means of which reconciliation would have to come. The purpose of the whole work can be summarized in two sentences from the last page: "First justice, then goodness; in the goodness, justice; and in the justice, goodness." And then the conclusion: "For every evil deed that has been done, we must work a deed of mercy; otherwise the wheel of cruelty will roll on."

Most of the attacks on Berggrav actually came from sources that had always been opposed to him or the things he stood for. Some critics wanted to hurt the Church through him; others wanted to hurt him because he had been one of the strongest leaders in the Resistance Movement. The suspicions circulated about him could infect others for a time because of the unstable state of mind that comes with a period of transition from war to peace and from occupation to freedom. But those who gave credence to the insinuations against him simply did not know Berggrav and his spontaneous reactions—in Schjelderup's words, again—"his warm humanity, his rich intellectual abilities, and first and last, his urge always to be useful."

Berggrav had taken these attacks to heart, especially because of the effect upon the Church. Therefore he was all the more grateful for the many ex-

pressions of friendship and sympathy that came to
him. When, because of a heart attack, he applied for
the Diocese of Hamar in 1946, he was pressed so
hard from all quarters to stay on as Bishop of Oslo
that he had to give in. During these last years he
was loved as few other men have been. He was
especially well known and respected abroad, having
been considered one of the greatest churchmen of
our time. His principal ecumenical achievements
were accomplished in the years after the War.

The Ecumenical Leader

M OST people don't even know what the word
ecumenical means," Berggrav once said at a
meeting. "But that doesn't matter. Two hundred
years ago nobody knew what *mission* meant either.
It, too, is a foreign word, and in fifty years the
word *ecumenical* will be just as dear to Christians
as the word *mission* is now."

The prophecy may be somewhat exaggerated;
but it is true that just as our missions are based on
the missionary commandment in Matthew 28, "Go
therefore and make disciples of all nations," so our
ecumenical work is based on the prayer of Jesus in
John 17:21, "that they may all be one."*

---

* The word *ecumenical* comes from the Greek *oikumene*, meaning
world. To Berggrav goes the credit for spelling our Norwegian form with
an *e*. Before the war, men spoke about the *økumeniske* work, with the
result that people were always confusing it with *økonomisk (economical)*
and so they thought it had something to do with church finance!

The ecumenical movement aims at making contacts among all the churches of the world, across all national borders and across all questions of church doctrine. Berggrav got into the work in earnest when he participated in the great ecumenical meeting at Stockholm in 1925. The dominating personality of that meeting was Archbishop Nathan Söderblom.

Berggrav in his eulogy of Bishop Bell of England said that it was Bell who "baptized me as an ecumenical." That is hardly right. Bell "confirmed" him at that time, in 1939; but it was Söderblom who baptized him and gave him faith in the ecumenical movement. His interest in it actually goes back even farther when he followed eagerly the founding of the Churches' League for Peace in 1914.

To begin with it was the practical aspects of the matter that interested Berggrav. Discussions about doctrines could come later; the problem then was, how can the churches work together to help the world in its need? In the years before the Second World War, he became chairman of the Churches' League for Peace and also chairman of the national committee of Norway. It was as chairman of the League for Peace that he undertook his attempts at peace-making in the winter of 1939-40. The summer before, the League held a big meeting at Larvik, Norway. The principal topic of discussion

at that time concerned the totalitarian state, and
Berggrav gave the main address on the subject.

As Bishop of Oslo he had also become chairman
of other Norwegian committees for ecumenical
work—the Committee on Faith and Order and
the Committee on Life and Work. Now the plan
was to let these various activities merge into a
World Council of Churches. A merger committee
had been at work since 1937. Berggrav was able to
unite the Norwegian committees into a Norwegian
Ecumenical Circle.

In February 1946 he was elected a member of the
committee on preparations for the World Council.
When the World Council of Churches was formal-
ly organized at Amsterdam in 1948, he became a
member of the Central Committee and later a
member of the Executive Committee, which has
relatively few members. In the meeting at Toronto
he was elected one of the presidents.

The general secretary of the World Council, Dr.
Visser't Hooft, in speaking of Berggrav's strenuous
committee work, says, "Berggrav played a great
part in the Council by creating an atmosphere of
mutual confidence. He became one of the shepherds
of the ecumenical movement, and he constantly reminded us of basic Biblical truths."

Berggrav was an ecumenical preacher as well as
a committee man.

At the first World Youth Conference held in Oslo in 1947, he officiated at the opening service in the Cathedral, where 1,400 young people from about 80 nations were gathered. The building was at that time undergoing extensive repairs, and it had only a temporary ceiling.

In breathless silence the young people heard him explain how God rules the world. "It is like the ceiling here in the church," he said, "which is lying oppressively heavy above all of us. But you must know that this is only a temporary ceiling which is laid because the artist must have something to stand on while he is redecorating the arch. We do not see the arch yet, because the artist is not finished. But just wait until this temporary ceiling is taken away and there will be a glorious sight before the eyes of all. So it is with God working in history. We can feel the oppressively low ceiling that He often lays over our lives. But we must realize that He is doing it only so that some day we shall see the completed arch in all its beauty!"

When he was about to pronounce the benediction from the altar a miscue occurred which Berggrav handled with characteristic tact and skill. He had begun by saying in a low voice, "I shall have to pronounce the benediction in Norwegian." The organist did not hear what he said and thought that it was the usual "The Lord be with you," and he

responded with the response for the congregation
"And With Thy Spirit." Then when Berggrav said,
"The Lord be with you," the organist set in with
his thundering threefold amen and the postlude.
I was in despair at the error, but Berggrav stood
there quietly. Finally the organ stopped. Now
Berggrav said in a loud voice, in English, "Sometimes it is that way in life—one has to wait for
God's benediction. But it *always comes.*" And then
it came, straight from Berggrav's lips to the hearts
of all those who were present.

When the Lutheran World Federation held its
constituting convention at Lund in 1947, the
relationship with the Germans was still strained
after the War. Berggrav surprised everyone by
giving his address in German and by speaking directly to the German delegates in such a tone and
manner as to melt the ice completely.

At the Lutheran World Convention at Hannover in 1952 he spoke on the subject *State and
Church* in such a way that nobody who was there
will forget it. It was then that he began by saying,
"There is a foe." He spoke about the demonic
danger that threatens the modern state, or nation.
So strong were his words that it was too much for
some of the strict Lutherans. Lutheranism has been
known at times to overemphasize obedience to gov-
ernmental authority, and now Berggrav went to the

other extreme so that a great argument developed within the whole German Church. In fact, a book on the subject has come out, beginning with Berggrav's address and including contributions by several leading German theologians. And good German Lutherans are still trying to repudiate Berggrav's ideas. They had a real sting because they were delivered by one who himself had fought such a demonic government, a government that had ruled with the help of German bayonets.

At the meeting of the World Council of Churches at Evanston, Illinois, the whole assembly paid homage to Berggrav by rising spontaneously after he had spoken. He had become something of a symbol in ecumenical work. "He belongs to all of us," said one of the leading churchmen of the United States. He created a sensation at this meeting by suggesting that a joint communion service be held, to be open to Christians from all faiths. The American Lutherans were in despair; for them it seemed essential to observe the distinction between the Lutheran concepts of communion and the concepts of the overwhelming majority of Reformed churches by which they are surrounded. Berggrav met with opposition on this point, but he took it with a smile. He was now seventy years old!

Berggrav was not only a man of words; he was also a man of action.

During a visit to a small Lutheran Church in
Paris which was working under difficult conditions,
he learned that the church had had to close its boys'
home, *Bon Secours* [Good Help], in one of the
city's poor sections. The home would have to be
completely renovated to be usable, and the church
had no money for the work.

Berggrav felt that here was an excellent opportunity for a Norwegian relief project. The job would
call for good unified effort in the Church at home,
but even more important was the fact that the
boys' home was one of the few pieces of social
service work the church in Paris could take care of.

Berggrav headed the drive in Norway, and Pastor Henry Dahl-Johannessen became the leader in
the practical work. Both money and furnishings
were collected. In the spring of 1953, Berggrav
donated his Goethe prize money to the boys' home.
The gift amounted to 10,000 German marks, or
about $2,500.00. The remodeled home was to be
done in pure Norwegian design and furnishing. It
was completed and dedicated in the fall of 1953,
with Berggrav present for the ceremony.

The Goethe Prize is awarded from a legacy at
Hamburg University in recognition of achievements conducive "to the promotion of international
thinking and humanitarian efforts." The two pre-
ceding years the prize had been awarded to inter-

nationally famous scientists; and the Rector who
presented the prize to Berggrav first gave an ap-
preciative survey of the Bishop's contributions to
science and then turned to his church work. His
concluding words are worthy of record:

"It is deplorable that it is so much easier for us
to notice what is mean than what is noble. What a
Quisling is we all know. We are now happy and
proud to be able to honor his opponent. And we
shall always remember in our hearts what a *Berggrav* is!"

At the death of Berggrav, General Secretary Visser't Hooft said, "He will be remembered among
us as a peacemaker, as a leader of the spiritual Resistance Movement, as a spiritual advisor and friend,
as a builder of the World Council of Churches, and
above all as a man of the Bible."

"The Bible" could be the heading for the last
and most important chapter in Berggrav's ecumenical work.

The chapter begins quite simply with his becoming, as Bishop of Oslo, the chairman of the Norwegian Bible Society. And this in turn led to his beginning on a new translation of the Bible during
his internment at Asker. "An Attempt at the Letter
to the Philippians" appeared in *Church and Culture*
in 1946. He also worked with the gospel of Mark.
His idea was to produce a translation for young

people in which the difficult wording and phrasing
of the Church Bible had been cleared away. After
the War he interested the Bible Society in the idea,
and work was begun on a translation for youth. He
was a member of the board of directors and rejoiced
when the work came out in print.

A long range plan for a new translation of the
Church Bible itself won his instant approval, and
as chairman of the main committee, he helped to
outline the undertaking.

However, he was to make his greatest contribution to another field of work with the Society.
Shortly after the Liberation, Dr. John R. Temple,
General Secretary of the British and Foreign Bible
Society, came to Oslo. He was making a round of
Europe to invite all Bible Societies to cooperate in
the work that needed to be done after the War. Dr.
Temple tells us about it. "There are times when
we feel absolutely certain that we are led by the
hand of God. I am thinking of a visit to Oslo in
1945. I shall never forget it. I was certain of divine
guidance when for the first time I met Bishop Berggrav."

The result was that a year later Berggrav took
part in a meeting of the Bible Societies at Elfinsward
in England. He reports on it as follows:

At Elfinsward I had to take a good many hard words from a
representative of one of the larger Bible societies. He said that

societies which are only providing Bibles for their own national areas are selfish societies. They have no heart for all the millions in the world who have no Bibles at all. At first I thought that the man was unjust. The fact was that we had done our duty in Norway. But his stern words proved to be a call from God. I came home and told my board that we were selfish and business minded, and that we lacked vision of the real purpose of the Bible. They were taken aback but not insulted. We got this idea: Up to that time, the London Society had been providing the Holy Scriptures for "our" island, our special missionary field, Madagascar. It was now our turn to relieve the Londoners of this burden and thus make it possible for them to take up the work somewhere else.

It was some time before the idea could be realized. But the Norwegian Bible Society was the first of the "selfish" societies to become mission minded. From that time on, the Bible Mission was the center of Berggrav's interests, and he gave much time to the cause. After his resignation [as Bishop of Oslo], in January of 1951, he became the leading emissary of the Bible Society. The last morning of his life, he drafted a letter to all who were to preach on Bible Mission Sunday, March 15, 1959.

Bible Sunday? I have the feeling that many of you have paused before this problem—"It is so hard for people to get anything out of Bible reading!" I was bothered by the problem myself for a long time, as if I were shy on behalf of the Bible. Then I received courage to forget my shyness. People *get* something out of reading this "difficult" book. It was best expressed perhaps by the African woman who said, "This book *reads* me." I recommend heartily that people read it.

The next problem? "There are so many good causes that

we have to ask our congregations to consider. Special offerings are not popular."

This cause, the Bible mission, the Bible for all peoples and tribes—this has priority because it concerns the foundation of all Christianity and because it is right *now* that is important. . . .

The letter was never finished. Just as it is quoted here, it lay on his desk when he died that afternoon. The Bible Mission is his last will and testament to our Church.

At the meeting at Elfinsward, Berggrav was elected to head negotiations for a world organization, and the next year he became the first president of the World Federation of Bible Societies. He led the organization until he declined reelection at the council meeting at Rio de Janeiro in 1957. He was weakened by illness when he went there, but he felt it his duty to meet with the group for this last time.

Berggrav had needed to utilize all his talents as leader of this large international organization. The Bible, as we know, each year sells more copies than any other book in the world. As president of the World Federation of Bible Societies, Berggrav was actually at the head of a number of the world's largest publishing houses, and his work dealt with immense sums of money and with great plans. If cooperation among the "big ones" got to creaking, the Bishop was the mediator, the authority, the friend—the one who could somehow manage to get everything working smoothly again.

In the *Manchester Guardian* for February 6, 1959, a contributor tells about a sermon Berggrav once gave in England about the Bible. "Bishop Berggrav used an unforgettable illustration. Once as a child when he was out in the woods he heard his father shout for him. Long before he could make out *what* his father was saying, he knew that *it was his father's voice*. So it is with the Bible: The main point is that in it God, our Father, is speaking, and knowing this is more important than the particular words."

When the oldest of all the Bible societies, the British and Foreign Bible Society, observed its 150th anniversary in 1954, Berggrav gave the opening address. It made a tremendous impression on the audience.

The longest and most solemn list of names of kings and princes to be found in the New Testament appears in the third chapter of Luke. Actually none of these names—with one exception—would be mentioned or known in the world today, had it not been for the one *event* which this roll of names introduces. As you hear the text now, note how the whole rank of mighty names reminds us of a regiment lined up as a guard of honor at a great event. These men have become famous only because of what happened while they were in office.

Here it is, just as Luke wrote it:

"In the fifteenth year of the *reign of Tiberius Caesar, Pon-*

tius Pilate being Governor of Judea, and *Herod* being tetrarch of Galilee, and his brother *Philip* tetrarch of the region of Itruraea and Trachonitis, and *Lysenias* tetrarch of Abilene, and in the high-priesthood of Annas and Caiaphas . . . "

That was the guard of honor. Now comes the great occasion they were waiting for: *"Then the Word of God came . . . "*

The Word of God is the sovereign before whom they bow— these rulers who appear here only once in the history of mankind. Not only is the scene unique, it affords a fabulous perspective. *This* sovereign was to live on through the history of all time, throughout all centuries, to this very day when we are assembled here at Central Hall.

One thousand and eight hundred years later the situation was this: In the year 1804, while Napoleon Bonaparte was emperor over most of the European continent, George III was king of Great Britain, Alexander was czar of Russia, and Thomas Jefferson was president of the United States—the Word of God came to a girl in Wales, by the name of Mary. Through her efforts in the midst of a world crisis, while Great Britain especially was threatened and shaken to her foundations, a society was organized in London that was given the name of "The British and Foreign Bible Society."

Today, one hundred and fifty years later, we ourselves— gathered as we are from many different parts of the world— are standing like a guard of honor, not primarily to congratulate this society, but together with the society as servants of God to proclaim, "The Word of God is coming—is coming to more and more peoples in more and more languages." The Word is on the march in 1954, and we bow before its majesty.

So Berggrav himself always stood at attention before the majesty of the Word of God. His devotion to it is evidenced even by the little guide that is slipped into all the Bibles that go out, beginning with the words, "Dear New Bible Reader!"

Through his work with the Bible Societies and with the ecumenical movement, Eivind Berggrav's name has become known throughout the world. It is a name that could open doors that would otherwise have remained closed. Only three Norwegians of our day have been internationally known during their lifetime—C. J. Hambro, Trygve Lie, and Eivind Berggrav. One of these international figures was a Churchman, probably for the first time in Norwegian Church history.

Berggrav found time to do some ecumenical work at home, too. In the Norwegian Ecumenical Circle there were some representatives from the free churches. Then in 1950 Berggrav founded the Contact Circle, composed of two representatives from the State Church to be appointed by the bishops, and two representatives from each of the free churches with nationwide scope. These included the Methodist Church, the Norwegian Baptist Society, the Norwegian Mission Union, the Norwegian Lutheran Free Church, and the Salvation Army. The purpose of the Circle was, according to its constitution, "With full understanding of the sincerity of our different confessions, the Contact Circle aims to provide for the expression of Christian fellowship that is present among us. In part we purpose to join together against possible attacks on our joint Christian faith, Christian morals, Christian philosophy, and Christian law-making; in part also to come together for deliberation on the status of Christianity in our country today. It is not, however, our purpose to start or support cooperation on a so-called 'alliance' basis."

The last point was unanimously augmented to read, "It is agreed that the item in the bylaws to the effect that the Circle is not to start or support Christian cooperation on the so-called 'alliance' basis is to be interpreted precisely as it reads, and that it is not intended to prevent individual members or bodies from occasionally taking part in meetings with people from other bodies. The Circle as such, however, is not to take part in such arrangements."

Berggrav's phrasing is to be noted both in the statement of purpose and in the addition to it. He attended the meetings eagerly to the very last. The Circle has now held thirty meetings and brought up for discussion a great number of timely questions, in the forefront among them the questions concerning instruction in Christianity in the grade schools. Typical of the spirit that prevails in the Circle is an exchange of pleasantries that was reported by Daniel Brændeland in a feature article in *Vårt Land* [*Our Country*, a Christian newspaper in Oslo], February 2, 1959. Two of the men from the Circle had just had a cup of coffee together and were on their way back to the meeting room. One of them was Berggrav. In his teasing way he said to the other, "We are so much in agreement that I think we should form a joint church body." To which the other replied, "No, Bishop, we are too late. That body was established almost 2,000 years ago!"

You can be sure that this reply was exactly to Berggrav's liking. He knew that there is really only one Church: the fellowship of all those who within all church bodies follow Christ and are "helplessly loyal to His Word." His ecumenical work was done with the hope of putting this belief into practice. This kind of Christianity is what the churches "are longing for," as he said in one of his books. For that was Jesus' own prayer: That they may all be one so that the world can believe.

How is one to evaluate the ecumenical effects of Berggrav's work at home and abroad?

Stephen Tschudi, a Norwegian pastor and writer, once gave an exaggerated but striking definition of an "ecumenist": "An 'ecumenist' is a person who, lacking fellowship with the Christians of his own church body, goes abroad to meet with like-minded persons from other church bodies." We cannot deny that this quip hits certain tendencies that have weakened the ecumenical movement. It has not been rooted firmly in the individual churches, and some of its men have made contacts quite easily with other church groups just because they lacked contacts with their own church.

But with Berggrav the opposite was true. Whether he was abroad or at home, he was genuinely Norwegian and genuinely Lutheran. Yet with him his firm anchorage in the Norwegian Church never created boundaries for him; it merely provided springboards to action. It was precisely as a Norwegian that he won hearts all over the world, and because he was so Lutheran at heart he could meet others "on the same wave length." He made people listen to what Norway had to offer, and he opened the eyes of men of other denominations to what Lutheranism could give to them. He became our best ambassador of the Lutheran church to the fellowship of churches everywhere.

There is no doubt either as to what was the common chord he had with others. Visser't Hooft hit it right when he spoke of Berggrav as a shepherd and a man of the Bible. His chief contribution was the clear, straight Biblical message that he could present with soul-searching understanding. Of course he was interested, too, in the administrative matters of the organizations he worked with, and he was a masterful diplomat in this field. But the influence that he had with others came not from his person but from what he represented—Christ's message from the Bible, proclaimed so simply and directly that people could understand it. Whether he was at Hurdal or Geneva or Rio, he always aimed at the hearts of people. And so he became not only one of the great church leaders of our time; he was an ecumenical messenger to the hearts of men.

Chapter Eleven

The Last Chapter

IN JUNE, 1946, it became evident that Berggrav's heart had not been equal to the strain put
upon it. He became seriously ill and had to take an
extended sick-leave. At that time he considered resigning from his post as Bishop of Oslo because he
thought that he would not be able to fill his position satisfactorily. The bishopric at Hamar had
become vacant at the death of Berggrav's good
friend, Bishop Hille. Berggrav then asked to be
transferred from Oslo to Hamar, where he believed
the load would be so much lighter that he would
be able to handle it. He placed first in the number
of votes for the position, but he was urged by people on all sides to remain in Oslo. Among other in-
ducements, the Government proposed a division of
the Oslo Diocese to lessen the burden of work.

So Berggrav continued as Bishop of Oslo until New Year, 1951. By that time it was evident to him that he could not continue in the office any longer. His heart trouble had occasioned several confinements at home or hospital, and he had to cancel a number of his official visits. So he felt obliged to resign.

This did not mean that he relaxed completely. In the years that followed, he was constantly on the go—except for his "interludes" in bed or in the hospital. He continued his ecumenical work, spent several months in the United States in 1954, giving a number of speeches here; and as we know, he went to Brazil in 1957 to the meeting of the World Federation of Bible Societies. Through his radio program at home he came into contact with a number of people—especially those who were troubled—and his correspondence became extensive. His days, too, were filled with consultations with people who wanted spiritual advice. He had become once more the pastor to those who were searching and longing for something. He was asked to speak at a number of meetings planned especially for such people. Berggrav never could say no. He should have done so, for his health grew steadily worse.

In 1954 he threw himself into the controversy over the relation between the Church and the State. People filled the old festival hall of the University

to hear the debate between him and Professor Castberg. The Radio Corporation broadcast the discussion and had to repeat it from tape some days later.

Although it was obvious that his strength was
dwindling, Berggrav's last year was a happy one.
He enjoyed living, even as he faced approaching
death with complete calm. His preaching was warm
and intimate, and he touched hearts as never before.
Fellowship with friends and family filled his life
to the brim. There was a blissful calmness over his
last days, a peaceful rounding out of what had
been a tension-filled life.

His death, which occurred late in the afternoon
of the fourteenth of January, 1959, was sudden, but
hardly unexpected. From his hand slipped a book
which he had been paging through; it was, charac-
teristically enough, a new edition of a work listing
his associates in the ministry, containing brief
sketches of the lives of men for whom he, lovingly,
had been a wise *pastor pastorum*.

Now at the close of Berggrav's saga, one may ask,
What was really the greatest thing about him?

After reading through the chapters on his work
as the scholar, the journalist, the church man, the
ecumenical leader, one answer seems obvious—his
versatility. He had such *breadth* of intensity.

But this, of course, is not the whole truth. His

real greatness was his *genuineness*. He was always himself. He became what he was destined to be. One noticed this quality most on meeting him face to face. Then all the clever versatility was forgotten; then he was a man—a fellow-man with you, and you sensed it in every nerve. He gave you that rare experience of feeling, "Here is a man who understands every inch of me." Many were the men who were privileged to know what it meant to come face to face with Bishop Berggrav.

It is perhaps most fitting to conclude with the words that he sent as a last greeting to his first parish. They appeared in print in the Christmas 1958 issue of the parish paper at Hurdal.

"We are getting old, many of us now. I was 74 this fall, and now I would be eligible for the parties for the old folks at Hurdal, as we had them in my time. But every Christmas I feel somehow younger, almost like a child. The difference comes from the fact that eternity is so much closer now. The busyness is over, the quiet is growing. The last Christmases I have spent at Øivind's, where there are five children and much Christmas! At times I think that my father and mother and especially Kathrine are there to rejoice with us.

"The smallest one in the house is two years old, and her name is Eva. She is especially loving to her grandfather, who is also, naturally, pretty fond of her. We two can play angels—she, a just-has-been one and I in the hope of about-to-be. Right now, neither of us is an angel. She has too much explosiveness in her; grandfather's supply of it has somewhat diminished, but not entirely so.

"And so I am sitting in my deep chair, not knowing whether this is my last Christmas. There is nothing sad about the thought. An old man with a life full of weeds and wounds—unbelievable as it sounds —has had imputed to him, by God, that which his Redeemer has done for him, and is graciously accepted as a child of God. This is what Christmas is —that God came to earth and took upon himself the condition of men so that we may attain to His. In the eyes of God both Eva and I are angels now. This is not to be fathomed. But it is to be *believed*.

"United in this faith we greet one another with wishes for a Christmas of joy!

> "Cordially,
> "Eivind Berggrav"

Bibliography

Krigerliv og religiøsitet. Oslo 1915.

Østlandsk reising (co-author, H. Koht). Oslo 1916.

Mannen Jesus. Oslo 1921.

De spør om de valgfrie? Oslo 1921.

Religionens terskel. Oslo 1924.

Ekumeniska mötet, en kontur. Stockholm 1925.

Den religiøse følelse i sundt sjeleliv. Oslo 1926.

Ensomhet og fellesskap i kristenlivet. Oslo 1928.

Spadestikk i kirkegrunn og kulturmark. Oslo 1929.

Fangens sjel og vår egen. Oslo 1929.

Brytningene omkring Olav og Stiklestad. Oslo 1930.

Nathan Söderblom. Oslo 1931.

Legeme og sjel i karakterliv og gudsliv. Oslo 1933.

Helliggjørelse. Oslo 1934.

Bibelhistorie for folkeskolen. Oslo 1935.

Harald Ostenfeld. København 1935.

Oxford—fanfar eller fåra? Stockholm 1935.

Elias Blix. Oslo 1936.

Fornyelsen av katekismen. Oslo 1936.

Ibsens sjelelige krise (co-author, Francis Bull). Oslo 1937.

Spenningens land. Oslo 1937.

(English translation by O. Herbert Aanestad: *Land of Suspense*, Augsburg Publishing House, Minneapolis, 1943.)

Svar på spørsmål om religion (several authors). Oslo 1937.

De store religioner (In *De tusen hjems bibliotek*, edited by Berggrav and a special article "Det hellige og kristendommen"). Oslo 1938.

Nordens innsats. Oslo 1939.

221

Katekismen med øvinger. Oslo 1939.

With God in the Darkness (Foreword by the Bishop of Chichester). London 1943.

Folkedommen over NS. Oslo 1945.

Da kampen kom. Oslo 1945.

Staten og mennesket. Oslo 1945.

(English translation by George Aus: *Man and State,* Muhlenberg Press, Philadelphia, 1951.)

Kirkens ordning i Norge. Oslo 1945.

The Norwegian Church in its international setting. London 1946.

Norske kirkeprofiler fra siste slektledd. Oslo 1946.

Tider og tekster. Oslo 1947.

Humor och allvar. Stockholm 1947. Norwegian edition, 1951.

Barnesjel og religion. Oslo 1949.

Kirkene lenges. Oslo 1952.

Contra Castberg. Oslo 1953.

Religionen og vi (over radio). Oslo 1953.

Kronprinsesse Märtha (illustrations with comments by Berggrav). Oslo 1955.

Marie Treschow. En livsskisse. Oslo 1955.

Mennesket Dronning Maud. Oslo 1956.

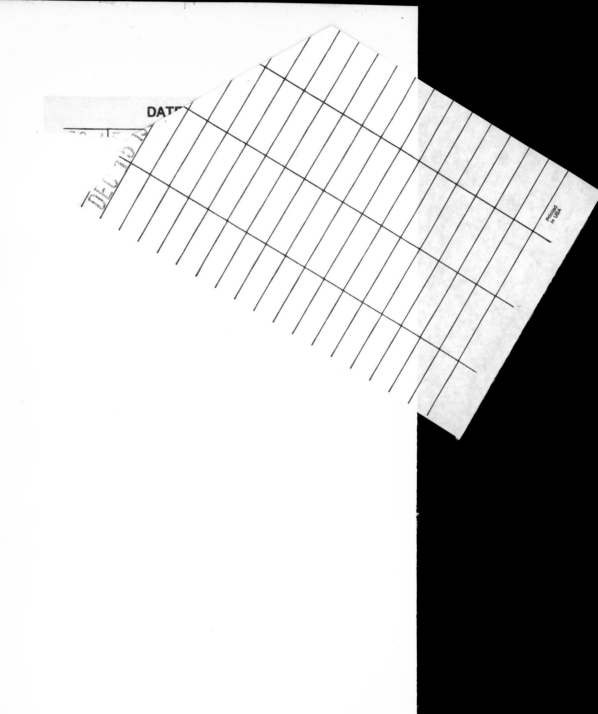

Printed in USA

to hear the debate between him and Professor Castberg. The Radio Corporation broadcast the discussion and had to repeat it from tape some days later.

Although it was obvious that his strength was
dwindling, Berggrav's last year was a happy one.
He enjoyed living, even as he faced approaching
death with complete calm. His preaching was warm
and intimate, and he touched hearts as never before.
Fellowship with friends and family filled his life
to the brim. There was a blissful calmness over his
last days, a peaceful rounding out of what had
been a tension-filled life.

His death, which occurred late in the afternoon
of the fourteenth of January, 1959, was sudden, but
hardly unexpected. From his hand slipped a book
which he had been paging through; it was, charac-
teristically enough, a new edition of a work listing
his associates in the ministry, containing brief
sketches of the lives of men for whom he, lovingly,
had been a wise *pastor pastorum*.

Now at the close of Berggrav's saga, one may ask,
What was really the greatest thing about him?

After reading through the chapters on his work
as the scholar, the journalist, the church man, the
ecumenical leader, one answer seems obvious—his
versatility. He had such *breadth* of intensity.

But this, of course, is not the whole truth. His

So Berggrav continued as Bishop of Oslo until New Year, 1951. By that time it was evident to him that he could not continue in the office any longer. His heart trouble had occasioned several confinements at home or hospital, and he had to cancel a number of his official visits. So he felt obliged to resign.

This did not mean that he relaxed completely. In the years that followed, he was constantly on the go—except for his "interludes" in bed or in the hospital. He continued his ecumenical work, spent several months in the United States in 1954, giving a number of speeches here; and as we know, he went to Brazil in 1957 to the meeting of the World Federation of Bible Societies. Through his radio program at home he came into contact with a number of people—especially those who were troubled—and his correspondence became extensive. His days, too, were filled with consultations with people who wanted spiritual advice. He had become once more the pastor to those who were searching and longing for something. He was asked to speak at a number of meetings planned especially for such people. Berggrav never could say no. He should have done so, for his health grew steadily worse.

In 1954 he threw himself into the controversy over the relation between the Church and the State. People filled the old festival hall of the University